Meeting The Little Prince

A Comprehensive Guide to the Little Prince

Johnny Wallman

Meeting The Little Prince
A comprehensive Guide to The Little Prince

'What makes a desert beautiful is that somewhere it hides a well.'

'I must endure the presence of a few caterpillars if I wish to become acquainted with the butterfies'

First published in United Kingdom in 2020

Copyright © Johnny Wallman 2020

jswallman@gmail.com

All rights reserved. No part of this publication may be reproduced without the written permission of the author.

Other novels from Johnny Wallman include;

Avalon Bed & Breakfast
Zahal: A Love Story, Life in the Israeli army
Nearly joined up writing ; A collection of random words
Johnny Wallman's Travel Bucket List 2019
Between The Rainbow and the Clouds

Meeting The Little Prince

Everything you wanted to know concerning the novel The Little Prince by Antoine de Saint-Exupéry but couldn't be bothered looking up on the internet.

All over the world there are dedications to Saint-Exupéry and The Little Prince. From Theme Parks to Statues, museums, streets, schools, mountains, wall murals, restaurants and more. So you find yourself on holiday in Paris, Madrid or New York, Tel Aviv, Quebec or almost anywhere in the world, there is something there, somewhere, sometimes hidden away, marking the memory of the novel The Little Prince.

Saint-Exupéry travelled extensively and left his mark. Years later the locals would mark his visit with some kind of memorial. This guide will help you follow his footsteps and find those memorials.

Meeting The Little Prince is a comprensive directory of all things Little Prince including:

Facts about the book The Little Prince
Facts about the author Antoine de Saint-Exupéry
The story of The Little Prince
Facts about the Exupery family
Details of monuments, parks and statues dedicated to Exupéry
Details of places of interest connected to The Little Prince
List of Little Prince translated languages and dialects
Honours and legacies to Antoine Saint-Exupéry
Little Prince in popular culture (film, music, theatre, opera)
Saint-Exupéry on world stamps
Celebrity endorsements and Quotes
List of books about The Little Prince and Saint-Exupéry

List of Spin off books from The Little Prince
Copyright ownership of The Little Prince

Introduction

The Little Prince is a novella by French aristocrat, writer, and aviator Antoine de Saint-Exupéry. It was first published in English and French in the US in April 1943, and posthumously in France following the liberation of France as Saint Exupéry's works had been banned by the Vichy Regime. The story tells of a young prince who visits several planets in space, including Earth. The story addresses themes of loneliness, friendship, love, and loss. Despite appearing as a children's book, The Little Prince makes importanmt observations about life, love, friendships and human nature. The Little Prince became Saint Exupéry's most successful work, selling over 150 million copies worldwide. It has been translated into over 350 languages and dialects. It has been adapted for two major movies, numerous plays worldwide, audio recordings, radio plays, television, ballet, and opera.

Finding The Little Prince

I was about fifteen or sixteen when I discovered two of my greatest loves, Van Morrison's album Astral Weeks and Antoine de Saint-Exupéry's The Little Prince. My friend Simon and myself were united in our angst against the world and our love of Manchester City. Like most teenagers we would hang around his bedroom listening to music and contriving the many ways we could piss off our parents. Simon lived two doors down the street and we would while away the hours encamped in his bedroom each relaxing on the two single beds.

It was during one of my many visits that I saw the light. Lying on one of the beds, Simon got up from the other bed and threw

me a book before walking over to his record player and putting on his new album Astral Weeks by Van Morrison.
'Read that and listen to this' he ordered.
I was memorised. For the next two hours I refused to move as I read the one hundred and nine pages of the book while the melodic tones of Van Morrison lifted me to a higher plane. It was dreamy, romantic before I had discovered romance and filled with fantastic images. I wanted to fly, to dance, to laugh and to cry. I wasn't lying on a single bed in Manchester, I was on Cypress Avenue. Meanwhile I read the book Simon had thrust into my life.

Quickly scanning The Little Prince one would belive the book is simply a cute children's story. Indeed the front cover gives no clue to the deep and clever insight the author has to human nature, love, friendship and what really is important in life. It just looks like another children's story. On reading the book everything changes. The old addage you can't tell a book by its cover has never been more relevant in The Little Prince. The author's message is brilliantly partly hidden throughout making the reader have to work it out, think about it. The book reminds us adults what is 'really' important in life, something we have forgotten over time. Chapter after chapter the book teaches us everything we should really already know. The Little Prince asks fundamental questions about our existence, the meaning of life. Yet, the answers the book gives never resort to religious absolution. The little prince teaches us lessons we have forgotten as we have grown up.

Numbers are not important. 'Grown-ups are very fond of numbers. When you tell them about a new friend, they never ask you the kind of questions that should be asked, such as: 'What kind of voice does he have?' 'What are his favourite games?' 'Does he collect butterflies?"Instead they ask: 'How old is he? How much money does his father earn?' They really do imagine this is the best way to discover what sort of person he is!'Look after the planet. 'It's a just a question of self-discipline,' the little prince explained later. 'First thing in the morning you look after yourself, you brush your teeth and wash your face, don't you? Well, the second thing you must do is to look after the planet.'

Relationships are important for a happy life. 'What exactly does 'tamed' mean?'
'Well, it's something too often forgotten,' said the fox. 'I suppose it means: to make some kind of relationship.'
'Relationship?'
'Yes,' said the fox. 'I'll explain. To me, you are just a just a little boy like any other, like a hundred thousand other little boys. I have no need of you and you have no need of me. To you I am a fox like any other, like a hundred thousand other foxes. But if you tame me, you and I, we will have created a relationship, and so we will need one another. You will be unique in the world for me… If you were to tame me, my whole life would be so much more fun. I would come to know the sound of your footstep, and it would be different from all the others. At the sound of any other footstep I would be down in my hole in the earth as quick as you like. But your footstep would be like music to my ears, and I would come running up out of my hole, quick as you like.'

The important things in life you cannot see with your eyes. The author gives countless beautiful and clever examples of hidden beauty. 'Draw me a sheep' where the final accepted sheep is hidden in a box. The prince's imagination, for he cannot see a sheep, allows him to imagine the one inside is the perfect sheep. The previous sheep drawn by the pilot could be seen by the Prince and were not acceptable for various reasons. 'Somewhere in the desert is hidden a well' where throughout the expanse of barren and harsh land is hidden the beauty of life sustaining water. Love may come with a certain amount of pain but it is worth it. However vain the rose may be, she still loves the prince and he loves her too, enough to put up with her faults.

Things can have different meanings for different people. 'Stars mean different things to different people. For travellers, stars tell them where they are, where they are going. For others, they are just little lights in the sky. For scholars, they are the world of the unknown, yet to be discovered and understood. For my businessman, they are gold. But all stars stay silent. And you? No one else in the world will see the stars as you do… For you, and only for you, the stars will always be laughing.'

The Book

The Little Prince First Original Edition

The Little Prince was first published in English by Reynal & Hitchcock, Inc. in New York on 6 April 1943 and, a few days later in French by the same publisher (Le Petit Prince). Both publications were hardcover books with 93 numbered pages, covered in cloth with a stamped a picture on the front cover and protected by a colour printed dust jacket. The first print run of the first edition only 525 copies (of which 25 were not for sale), all numbered and autographed by the author, were printed from the first print run of the original first English language edition. Only 260 copies (of which 10 were not for sale) came out of press from the first print run of the first edition in French language; these were also all numbered and autographed by the author.

The story begins with grown-ups and their inability to understand what is important anymore. As a test to determine if a grown-up still thinks like a child, he shows them a picture that he drew when he was six years old depicting a snake which has eaten an elephant. If the grown-ups reply that the picture depicts a hat he knows that the grown up is too grown up and has lost that childhood innocence and naivity. The narrator becomes a pilot and one day, his plane crashes in the Sahara far from civilization. He has only eight days of water and must fix his airplane to be saved. From nowhere a young boy, the little prince appears. The prince, with golden hair, keeps repeating questions to the pilot until they are answered. The little prince asks him to draw a sheep. The narrator first shows him his old picture of the elephant inside the snake, which, to the narrator's surprise, the prince interprets correctly. After three failed attempts at drawing a sheep, the frustrated narrator simply draws a box claiming that the sheep the prince wants is inside the box. Again, to the narrator's surprise, the prince exclaims that this was exactly the drawing he wanted. Over the course of eight days stranded in the desert, while the narrator attempts to repair his plane, the little prince recounts the story of his life.

The prince tells of life on his tiny home planet, a small asteroid known as B612. The asteroid's most prominent features are three minuscule volcanoes (two active, and one dormant) as well as a variety of plants. He describes spending his earlier days cleaning the volcanoes and weeding unwanted seeds and sprigs that infest his planet's soil and in particular, pulling out baobab trees that are constantly on the verge of overrunning the planet. The prince wants a sheep to eat the undesirable plants, but worries it will also eat plants with thorns. The prince tells of his love for a vain rose that began growing on the asteroid. The rose is very pretensious and seeking attention. The prince says he nourished the rose and attended her, making a screen or glass globe to protect her from the cold wind, watering her, and keeping off the caterpillars. Although the prince fell in love with the rose, he also began to feel that she was taking advantage of him and he decided to leave the planet to explore the rest of the universe. Upon their goodbyes, the rose apologizes that she failed to show she loved him. She wishes him well and turns down his desire to leave her in the glass globe, saying she will protect herself. The prince worries that she will be unprotected while he is away, even with her thorns.

The prince visits six other planets before arriving at Earth. Each planet is inhabited by a single, irrational and narrow-minded adult, each relating to an element of society. The planets include:
A king with no subjects, who only issues orders that can be

followed, such as commanding the sun to set at sunset. A narcissistic man who only wants the praise which comes from admiration and being the most-admirable person on his otherwise uninhabited planet. A drunkard who drinks to forget the shame of drinking. A businessman who is blind to the beauty of the stars and instead endlessly counts and catalogues them in order to 'own' them all. A lamplighter on a planet so small, a full day lasts a minute. He wastes his life blindly following orders to extinguish and relight the lamppost every 30 seconds to correspond with his planet's day and night. An elderly geographer who has never been anywhere, or seen any of the things he records.

Because the prince landed in a desert, he first thought that Earth was uninhabited. He met a yellow snake that claimed to have the power to return him to his home, if he ever wished to return. The prince next met a desert flower, who told him that she had only seen a handful of men in this part of the world and that they had no roots, letting the wind blow them around and living hard lives. After climbing the highest mountain he had ever seen, the prince hoped to see the whole of Earth, thus finding the people; however, he saw only the enormous, desolate landscape. When the prince called out, his echo answered him, which he interpreted as the voice of a boring person who only repeats what another says.

The prince encountered a whole row of rosebushes, becoming downcast at having once thought that his own rose was unique and that she had lied. He began to feel that he was not a great prince at all, as his planet contained only three tiny volcanoes and a flower that he now thought of as common. He lay down on the grass and wept, until he met a fox. The fox desired to be tamed and teaches the prince how to tame him. By being tamed, something goes from being ordinary and just like all the others, to be special and unique. There are drawbacks since the connection can lead to sadness and longing when apart. From the fox, the prince learns that his rose was indeed unique and special because she was the object of the prince's love and time; he had "tamed" her, and now she was more precious than all of the roses he had seen in the garden. Upon their sad departing, the fox imparts a secret: important things can only be seen with the heart, not the eyes. The prince finally meets two people from Earth. A railway switchman who told him how passengers constantly rushed from one place to another aboard trains, never satisfied with where they were and not knowing what they were after while only the children among them ever bothered to look out the windows. A merchant who talked to the prince about his product, a pill that eliminated the need to drink for a week, saving people 53 minutes.

On the eighth day after the narrator's plane crash and the narrator and the prince are dying of thirst. The prince has become visibly morose and saddened over his recollections and longs to return home and see his flower. The prince finds a well, saving them. The narrator later finds the prince talking to the snake, discussing his return home and his desire to see his rose again, whom he worries has been left to fend for herself. The prince bids an emotional farewell to the narrator and states that if it looks as though he has died, it is only because his body was too heavy to take with him to his planet. The prince warns the narrator not to watch him leave, as it will upset him. The narrator, realizing what will happen, refuses to leave the prince's side. The prince consoles the narrator by saying that he only need look at the stars to think of the prince's lovable laughter, and that it will seem as if all the stars are laughing. The prince then walks away from the narrator and allows the snake to bite him, soundlessly falling down. The next morning, the narrator is unable to find the prince's body. He finally manages to repair his airplane and leave the desert. It is left up to the reader to determine if the prince returned home, or died. The story ends with a drawing of the landscape where the prince and the narrator met and where the snake took the prince's corporeal life. The narrator requests to be immediately contacted by anyone in that area encountering a small person with golden curls who refuses to answer any questions.

Some believe that the prince's kindhearted but petulant and vain rose was inspired by Saint Exupéry's wife. with the small home planet being inspired by her small native country, El Salvador, also known as 'The Land of Volcanoes'. Despite a tumultuous marriage, Saint Exupéry kept Consuelo close to his heart and portrayed her as the prince's rose, whom he tenderly protects with a wind screen and places under a glass dome on his tiny planet. Saint Exupéry's infidelity and the doubts of his marriage are perhaps symbolized by the vast field of roses the prince encounters during his visit to Earth.
This interpretation was described by biographer Paul Webster who stated she was 'the muse to whom Saint Exupéry poured out his soul in copious letters..... Consuelo was the rose in The Little Prince. I should have judged her by her acts and not by her words,' says the prince. 'She wrapped herself around me and enlightened me. I should never have fled. I should have guessed at the tenderness behind her poor ruses'.

Saint-Exupéry may have drawn inspiration for the prince's character and appearance from his own self as a youth, as during his early years friends and family called him the Sun King because of his golden curly hair. The author had also met a precocious eight-year-old with curly blond hair while he was residing with a family in Quebec City in 1942. Another possible inspiration for the little prince has been suggested as Land Morrow Lindbergh, the young, golden-haired son of fellow aviator Charles Lindbergh whom he met during an overnight stay at their Long Island home in 1939.When Life photojournalist John Phillips questioned the author-aviator on his inspiration for the child character, Saint- Exupéry told him that one day he looked down on what he thought was a blank sheet and saw a small childlike figure: 'I asked him who he was,' he replied. 'I'm the Little Prince'.

The original 140-page manuscript of The Little Prince, along with various drafts and trial drawings, were acquired from the author's close friend Silvia Hamilton in 1968 by curator Herbert Cahoon of the Pierpont Morgan Library, New York City. It is the only known surviving handwritten draft of the complete work. The manuscript's pages include large amounts of the author's prose that was not published as part of the first edition. In addition to the manuscript, several illustrations by the author are also held by the museum. They were not part of the first edition. The institution has marked both the 50th and 70th anniversaries of the novella's publication, along with the centenary celebration of the author's birth, with major exhibitions of the authors literary works.

The story's keynote definition 'One sees clearly only with the heart. What is essential is invisible to the eye' was reworded and rewritten some 15 times before achieving its final phrasing. His initial 30,000-word working manuscript was distilled to less than half its original size through laborious editing sessions. Multiple versions of its many pages were created and its prose then polished over several drafts, with the author occasionally telephoning friends in the middle of the night to solicit opinions on his newly written passages.

Many pages and illustrations were cut from the finished work as he sought to maintain a sense of ambiguity to the story's theme and messages. Deleted pages described the prince's vegetarian diet and the garden on his home asteroid that included beans, radishes, potatoes and tomatoes, but which lacked fruit trees that might have overwhelmed the prince's planet. Deleted chapters discussed visits to other asteroids occupied by a retailer brimming with marketing phrases, and an inventor whose creation could produce any object desired at a touch of its controls. Likely the result of the ongoing war in Europe weighing on Saint- Exupéry's shoulders, the author produced a sombre three-page epilogue lamenting 'On one star someone has lost a friend, on another someone is ill, on another someone is at war...', with the story's pilot-narrator noting of The Prince: 'he sees all that. . . . For him, the night is hopeless. And for me, his friend, the night is also hopeless.' The draft epilogue was also omitted from the novella's printing.

Saint Exupéry met Leon Werth , a writer and art critic, in 1931. Werth soon became **Saint-Exupéry's** closest friend outside of his work associates. Werth was an anarchist, a leftist Bolshevik supporter of Jewish descent and over twenty years older than Saint Exupéry.

Saint- Exupéry dedicated two books to him. At the beginning of the Second World War while writing The Little Prince Saint-Exupéry lived in his downtown New York City apartment, thinking of his native France and his friends. Werth spent the war unobtrusively in his village in a mountainous region near Switzerland where he was 'alone, cold and hungry' After the Fall of France during its occupation, the Werths remained in France despite offers by the Centre americain de secours in Marseille to help them emigrate. In July 1941 Werth was required to register as Jewish, his travel was restricted and his works banned from publication. His wife, Suzanne, was active in the Resistance, crossing the demarcation line clandestinely more than a dozen times and establishing their Paris apartment as a safe house for fugitive Jewish women, downed British and Canadian pilots, secret resistance meetings and storage of false identity papers and illegal radio transmitters.

To Leon Werth
I ask children to forgive me for dedicating this book to a grown-up. I have a serious excuse: this grown-up is the best friend I have in the world. I have another excuse: this grown-up can understand everything, even books for children. I have a third excuse: he lives in France where he is hungry and cold. He needs to be comforted. If all these excuses are not enough then I want to dedicate this book to the child whom this grown-up once was. All grown-ups were children first. (But few of them remember it.) So I correct my dedication:
To Leon Werth,
When he was a little boy

Saint-Exupéry's aircraft disappeared over the Mediterranean in July 1944. The following month, Werth learned of his friend's disappearance from a radio broadcast. Without having yet heard of The Little Prince, in November, Werth discovered that Saint-Exupéry had published a fable the previous year in the U.S., which he had illustrated himself, and that it was dedicated to him. At the end of the Second World War, which Antoine de Saint-Exupéry did not live to see, Werth said: 'Peace, without Tonio (Saint Exupéry) isn't entirely peace.' Werth did not see the text for which he was so responsible until five months after his friend's death, when Saint-Exupéry's French publisher sent him a special edition. Werth died in Paris in 1955.

Many of the book's initial reviewers were confused by the multi-layered story line and its morals, perhaps expecting a significantly more conventional story from one of France's leading writers. Its publisher had anticipated such reactions to a work that fell neither exclusively into a children's nor adult's literature classification. The New York Times reviewer wrote shortly before its publication 'What makes a good children's book?...... ...The Little Prince which is a fascinating fable for grown-ups of conjectural value for boys and girls of 6, 8 and 10. It may very well be a book on the order of Gullivers Travels,something that exists on two levels'; 'Can you clutter up a narrative with paradox and irony and still hold the interest of 8 and 10-year olds?' Notwithstanding the story's duality, the review added that major portions of the story would probably still 'capture the imagination of any child.' Addressing whether it was written for children or adults, the publishers promoted it ambiguously, saying that as far as they were concerned "it's the new book by Saint- Exupéry', adding to its dustcover 'There are few stories which in some way, in some degree, change the world forever for their readers. This is one.'

The book enjoyed modest initial success, residing on The New York Times Best Seller List for only two weeks, as opposed to his earlier 1939 English translation, Wind Sand and Stars which remained on the same list for nearly five months. As a cultural icon, the novella regularly draws new readers and reviewers, selling almost two million copies annually. Katherine Woods produced the first English translation of 1943, which was later joined by several other English translations. Her translation contained some errors.Mistranslations aside, one reviewer noted that Wood's almost poetic English translation has long been admired by many Little Prince lovers, who have spanned generations. As of 2019 at least seven additional English translations have been published.

My Favourite Quotes

'You become responsible, forever, for what you have tamed.'

'But the conceited man did not hear him. Conceited people never hear anything but praise.'

'Well, I must endure the presence of a few caterpillars if I wish to become acquainted with the butterflies.'

'Where are the people?' resumed the little prince at last. 'It's a little lonely in the desert…It is lonely when you're among people, too' said the snake.

'A rock pile ceases to be a rock pile the moment a single man contemplates it, bearing within him the image of a cathedral.'

'I have lived a great deal among grown-ups. I have seen them intimately, close at hand. And that hasn't much improved my opinion of them.'

'Only the children know what they are looking for.'

"But the eyes are blind. One must look with the heart."

'All men have stars, but they are not the same things for different people. For some, who are travelers, the stars are guides. For others they are no more than little lights in the sky. For others, who are scholars, they are problems... But all these stars are silent. You-You alone will have stars as no one else has them.'

'And now here is my secret, a very simple secret: It is only with the heart that one can see rightly; what is essential is invisible to the eye.'

'It is much more difficult to judge oneself than to judge others. If you succeed in judging yourself rightly, then you are indeed a man of true wisdom.'

'All grown-ups were once children... but only few of them remember it.'

'It is the time you have wasted for your rose that makes your rose so important.'

'The most beautiful things in the world cannot be seen or touched, they are felt with the heart.'

'No one is ever satisfied where he is.'

'One day, I watched the sun setting forty-four times......You know...when one is so terribly sad, one loves sunsets.'

'People where you live," the little prince said, "grow five thousand roses in one garden... Yet they don't find what they're looking for... And yet what they're looking for could be found in a single rose.'

'It is such a mysterious place, the land of tears.'

'What makes the desert beautiful,' said the little prince, 'is that somewhere it hides a well...'

'Grown-ups never understand anything by themselves, and it is tiresome for children to be always and forever explaining things to them.'

'The proof that the little prince existed is that he was charming, that he laughed, and that he was looking for a sheep. If anybody wants a sheep, that is a proof that he exists.'

'To forget a friend is sad. Not everyone has had a friend.'

'Words are the source of misunderstandings.'

'Men have no more time to understand anything. They buy ready-made things in the shops. But since there are no shops where you can buy friends, men no longer have any friends.'

'Sometimes, there is no harm in putting off a piece of work until another day.'

'It's all a great mystery...Look up at the sky and you'll see how everything changes.'

'If you love a flower which happens to be on a star, it is sweet at night to gaze at the sky. All the stars are a riot of flowers.'

'Grown ups are certainly very strange.'

'Of course I love you. It is my fault that you have not known it all the while.'

'And when your sorrow is comforted (time soothes all sorrows) you will be content that you have known me.'

'Look up at the sky. Ask yourself, "Has the sheep eaten the flower or not?" And you'll see how everything changes. . . . And no grown-up will ever understand how such a thing could be so important.'

The Author

Saint- Exupéry was born in Lyon to an aristocratic Catholic family that could trace its lineage back several centuries. He was the third of five children of the Viscountess Marie de Fonscolombe and Viscount Jean de **Saint-Exupéry** 1863–1904. His father, an executive of the The Sun insurance brokerage, died of a stroke in Lyon's La Foux train station before his son's fourth birthday. His father's death affected the entire family, transforming their status to that of 'impoverished aristocrats'. Saint Exupéry had three sisters and a younger blond-haired brother, François, who at age 15 died of rheumatic fever contracted while both were attending the Marianist College Villa St Jean in Fribourg, Switzerland during World War I. Saint-Exupéry attended to his brother, his closest confidant, beside François' death bed, and later wrote that François '...remained motionless for an instant. He did not cry out. He fell as gently as a [young] tree falls', imagery which would much later be recrafted into the climactic ending of The Little Prince. At the age of 17, now the only man in the family following the death of his brother, the young author was left as distraught as his mother and sisters, but he soon assumed the mantle of a protector and took to consoling them.

After twice failing his final exams at a preparatory Naval Academy, **Saint-Exupéry** entered the Ecole des Beaux-Arts as an auditor to study architecture for 15 months, again without graduating, and then fell into the habit of accepting odd jobs. In 1921, **Saint-Exupéry** began his military service as a basic-rank soldier with the 2nd Regiment of light cavalry and was sent to Neuhof, near Strasbourg. While there he took private flying lessons and the following year was offered a transfer from the French Army to the French Air Force. He received his pilot's wings after being posted to the 37th Fighter Regiment in

Casablanca, Morocco. Later, being reposted to the 34th Aviation Regiment on the outskirts of Paris, and then experiencing the first of his many plane crashes **Saint-Exupéry** Exupéry bowed to the objections of the family and left the air force to take an office job. He worked at several more odd jobs without success over the next few years. By 1926, Saint-Exupéry was flying again. He became one of the pioneers of international postal flight in the days when aircraft had few instruments. Later he complained that those who flew the more advanced aircraft had become more like accountants than pilots. In 1929, Saint- Exupéry was transferred to Argentina, where he was appointed director of the Aeroposta Argentina airline. He surveyed new air routes across South America, negotiated agreements, and even occasionally flew the airmail as well as search missions looking for downed fliers.

Saint-Exupéry's first novella, The Aviator was published in 1926 in a short-lived literary magazine. In 1929, his first book Southern Mail was published; his career as an aviator and journalist was about to begin. Publication of Night Flight established Saint-Exupéry as a rising star in the literary world. It was the first of his major works to gain widespread acclaim. That same year Saint-Exupéry married Consuelo Suncin a once-divorced, once-widowed Salvadoran writer and artist. Saint-Exupéry, thoroughly enchanted by the diminutive woman, would leave and then return to her many times. It was a stormy union, with Saint-Exupéry travelling frequently and indulging in numerous affairs, most notably with the Frenchwoman Hélène de Vogüé . Vogüé became Saint-Exupéry's literary executor after his death and also wrote her own Saint-Exupéry biography under a pseudonym, Pierre Chevrier. Saint-Exupéry continued to write until the spring of 1943, when he left the United States with American troops bound for North Africa in the Second World War.

On 30 December 1935, at 2:45am, after 19 hours and 44 minutes in the air, Saint-Exupéry, along with his mechanic-navigator André Prévot, crashed in the Libyan desert during an attempt to break the speed record in a Paris-to-Saigon air race and win a prize of 150,000 francs. Both Saint-Exupéry and Prévot miraculously survived the crash, only to face rapid dehydration in the intense desert heat. Their maps were primitive and ambiguous, leaving them with no idea of their location. The pair had only one day's worth of fluids. They both saw mirages and experienced auditory hallucinations, which were quickly followed by more vivid hallucinations. By the second and third day, they were so dehydrated that they stopped sweating. On the fourth day, a Bedouin on a camel discovered them and administered a native rehydration treatment that saved their lives. The near brush with death would figure prominently in his 1939 memoir, Wind, Sand and Stars. Saint-Exupéry's classic The Little Prince. which begins with a pilot being stranded in the desert, is, in part, a reference to this experience. After France's armistice with Germany Saint-Exupéry went into exile in North America, escaping through Portugal. He arrived in New York City on the last day of 1940, with the intention of convincing the U.S. to enter the conflict against Nazi Germany quickly. Between January 1941 and April 1943, the Saint-Exupérys lived in New York City's Central Park South in twin penthouse apartments as well as The Bevin House mansion on Long Island and a townhouse in Manhattan.

It was after Saint-Exupéry's arrival in the United States that the author adopted the hyphen within his surname, as he was annoyed with Americans addressing him as 'Mr. Exupéry'. It was also during this period that he authored Flight to Arras which earned widespread acclaim, and Letter to a Hostage, dedicated to the 40 million French living under Nazi rule plus numerous shorter pieces in support of France. The Saint-Exupérys also resided in Quebec City, Canada for several weeks during the late spring of 1942, during which time they met a precocious eight-year-old boy with blond curly hair, Thomas, the son of philosopher Charles De Koninck with whom the Saint-Exupérys resided. After he returned from his stay in Quebec, which had been fraught with illness and stress, the French wife of one of his publishers helped persuade Saint-Exupéry to produce a children's book hoping to calm his nerves. Saint-Exupéry wrote and illustrated The Little Prince in New York City in mid-to-late 1942, with the manuscript being completed in October. It would be first published months later in early 1943 in both English and French in the United States, and would only later appear in his native homeland posthumously after the liberation of France as his works had been banned by the collaborationist Vichy Regime.

In April 1943, following his 27 months in North America, Saint-Exupéry departed with an American military convoy for Algiers to fly with the Free French Air Force and fight with the Allies in a Mediterranean-based squadron. Then 43, soon to be promoted to the rank of commandant (major), he was far older than most men in operational units. Although eight years over the age limit for such pilots, he had petitioned endlessly for an exemption which had finally been approved by General Dwight Eisenhower. However, Saint-Exupéry had been suffering pain and immobility due to his many previous crash injuries, to the extent that he could not dress himself in his own flight suit or even turn his head leftwards to check for enemy aircraft.

After Saint-Exupéry resumed flying, he also returned to his longtime habit of reading and writing while flying his single seat F-5B. On one flight, to the chagrin of his colleagues awaiting his arrival, he circled the airport for an hour after returning, so that he could finish reading a novel. Saint-Exupéry frequently flew with a lined notebook during his long solitary flights and some of his philosophical writings were created during such periods when he could reflect on the world below him. Prior to his return to flight duties with his squadron in North Africa, the collaborationist Vichy Regime unilaterally promoted Saint-Exupéry as one of its members – quite a shock to the author. Subsequently, French General (later French President Charles de Gaulle whom Saint-Exupéry and others held in low regard, publicly implied that the author-pilot was supporting Germany. Depressed at this, he began to drink heavily. Additionally, his health, both physically and mentally, had been deteriorating. Saint-Exupéry was said to be intermittently subject to depression and there was discussion of taking him off flying status.

Saint-Exupéry's last assigned reconnaissance mission was to collect intelligence on German troop movements in and around the Rhone Valley preceding the Allied invasion of France. Although he had been reinstated to his old squadron with the provision that he was to fly only five missions, on 31 July 1944, he took off on his ninth reconnaissance mission from an airbase on Corsica. To the great alarm of the squadron compatriots who revered him, he did not return, vanishing without a trace. Word of his disappearance shortly spread across the literary world and then into international headlines. An unidentifiable body in a French uniform was found several days after his disappearance south of Marseille and buried in Carqueiranne in September. In September 1998, to the east of Riou Island (south of Marseille) fisherman Jean-Claude Bianco found a silver identity bracelet bearing the names of Saint-Exupéry, his wife Consuelo and his American publisher. The recovery of his bracelet was an emotional event in France, where Saint-Exupéry had by then assumed the mantle of a national icon and some disputed its authenticity as it was found far from his intended flight path, implying that the aircraft might not have been shot down.

In May 2000, Luc Vanrell, a diver, found the partial remains of a Lockheed P-38 Lightning on the seabed off the coast of Marseille, near where the bracelet was previously found. The discovery galvanized the country, which for decades had conducted searches for his aircraft and speculated on Saint-Exupéry's fate. After a two-year delay imposed by the French government, the remnants of the aircraft were recovered in October 2003. On 7 April 2004, Patrick Granjean, head of the French Ministry of Culture and investigators confirmed that the remnants of the crash wreckage were, indeed, from Saint-Exupéry's plane. No marks or holes attributable to gunfire were found; however, that was not considered significant as only a small portion of the aircraft was recovered. The location of the crash site and the bracelet are less than 80km by sea from where the unidentified French serviceman was found and it remains plausible, but has not been confirmed, that the body was carried there by sea currents after the crash over the course of several days.

While not precisely autobiographical, much of Saint-Exupéry's work is inspired by his experiences as a pilot.
Saint-Exupéry's notable literary works are
1926 The Aviator
1929 Southern Mail
1931 Night Flight
1938 The Wild Garden
1939 Wind, Sand and Stars
1942 Flight to Arras
1943 The Little Prince
1944 Letter to a Hostage

Antoine de Saint Exupery Timeline

1904 After the Viscount died, Marie moved with her five children to the Castle of Saint-Maurice-de-Remens, northeast of Lyon.

1909, the family moved to the home of Antoine's paternal grandfather in Le Mans, in central France Antoine de Saint-Exupéry arrived in Sarthe at the age of 9, a few years after the death of his father. He lived five years in Le Mans, from 1909 to 1914, in a bourgeois house in the city center, with his mother and brother. Saint Exupéry and his younger brother, Francois, started attending the Jesuit school of Notre Dame de Montgré at Villafrance, near Lyon.

1915 November, as the war grew worse, the two brothers moved to the Villa Saint-Jean school in Fribourg, Switzerland

1918, June he entered the School of Fine Arts in Paris and studied architecture for fifteen months.

1921, April Saint Exupéry began his required two years of French military service. He went to Nuehof, Strasbourg, in southeastern France, for training as a pilot.

1921, December 1921, he obtained his military pilot's license and then served briefly in Casablanca, Morocco in North Africa.

1922, Saint-Exupéry then returned to Paris, where he fell in love with Louise de Vilmorin.

1926, October Saint-Exupéry began flying for the Latecoêre Line based in Toulouse. He flew the mail through France, Spain, and northern Africa.

1927, He started spending much of his time in Dakar, Senegal, and began learning about the Sahara desert and its people

1929, Saint-Exupéry published his first novel, Courrier Sud, or Night Mail. That same year, he moved to South America and quickly became director of an airmail company called Aeroposta Argentina

1935, December flight, Saint-Exupéry and his navigator Andre Prevot crashed their plane in the Sahara desert at Wadi Natrun, near the Nile Delta. The aviator walked in the desert for a few days before being rescued by a Bedouin caravan.

1936, He returned to his writing life and covered the May Day events in Moscow. That same year, war returned to Europe in the form of the Spanish Civil War.

1937, Saint-Exupéry returned to flying, having bought a Caudron Simon aircraft to replace the one that he had lost in the Sahara. A year later, he crashed again, this time in Guatemala, and suffered injuries from which he never fully recovered.

1939, September 1, 1939, World War II began when Germany invaded Poland, and then Great Britain and France declared war on Germany. Saint-Exupéry, despite his flight injuries, joined the French air force to fly reconnaissance missions.

1940 December, German forces had already overwhelmed the French and entered Paris. Saint-Exupéry had joined the Free

French forces, but his air squadron eventually was demobilized. The flier escaped from France and eventually made his way to New York City, where he first lived in Manhattan near the southwest corner of Central Park.

1942 With France still under control of Nazi Germany, Saint-Exupéry had moved into a house in Asharoken, on Long Island's north shore. While living there, he started writing and illustrating a children's book based on his earlier flying exploits

1944, July 31, he took off from an Allied airbase in Borgo, Corsica, headed for the Grenoble region in southern France to take reconnaissance photos. His plane disappeared that same day. His squadron declared him officially missing on September 8.

1972 Saint-Exupéry mother outlived her son and died aged 92.

1979 His widow, Consuelo, died. She is buried in the famous Pere-LaChaise cemetery in Paris, next to her first husband.

The Saint-Exupery Family

Jean de Saint-Exupéry (1863-1904)

Jean de Saint-Exupéry, was first a dragon officer, then out of necessity, joined the paternal insurance company which sent him to Lyon. At 33, after having "thrown away his flair", he was an attractive and distinguished gentleman, a beautiful name who had little fortune and a taste for pleasure, in short, he was a true 'French knight. At the home of a distant relative, the Countess of Tricaud, he met Marie de Fonscolombe, fresh out of the Sacré-Coeur of Lyon where she was raised, torn from her native Provence. He married her on June 8, 1896 and the couple moved to Lyon, a stone's throw from Place Bellecour. Jean died suddenly, at the age of 41, of a stroke in La Foux station. Antoine's parents were married at Saint-Maurice. His father Jean and his only brother Francois were buried there.

Marie Boyer de Fonscolombe (1875-1972)

Married to Jean de Saint-Exupéry, Marie lived in Lyon and led the life of a young woman of her time and her community. In seven years of marriage, five children succeed one another: Marie-Madeleine (1897),Simone (1898), Antoine (1900), François (1902), Gabrielle (1903). In the summer of 1904, she su ddenly became a widow and never remarried. The first days of her widowhood, she lived at La Mole, with her parents, then moved to Lyon with Tante Tricaud. She did not settle anywhere with multiplie stays with her parents, brothers and cousins. In this rather difficult nomadic life, she carefully followed the education of her children.

During the First War, she created an infirmary at Ambérieu

station under the aegis of the Red Cross. When Aunt Tricaud died in 1920, she inherited the Château de Saint-Maurice where she settled. Although her income was very modest, she provided for her children but had to sell the land adjoining the castle. Her free time, she painted and in 1922, she was received at the Salon d'Automne by French artists. She had talent, institutions and individuals acquired her paintings. When her daughter Marie-Madelaine died in 1927, she returned to the Red Cross, which entrusted her with a mission in a village in the Somme, then in Normandy. She returned to Saint-Maurice in 1928, she assisted the poorest in Lyon, treated cancer patients with the Dames du Calvaire. In 1932, she sold the Saint-Maurice property, which had become too large and too cumbersome to manage. She moved to Cannes before buying a house in Cabris which she named Les Fioretti, in tribute to her son François, where she would spend the rest of her life. When France went to war, she was admitted as a volunteer nurse at the Vallauris hospital. And at the time of the shelling of the coast, she welcomed Gabrielle and her family home. In August 1944, when she learned of Antoine's disappearance, she took refuge in prayer. She wrote poems where she often talked about her son. At the beginning of the 1960s, she gradually lost her sight before dying on February 2nd 1972 at Cabris, Alpes-Maritimes, Provence-Alpes-Côte d'Azur, France

François, known as The Quiet Father (1902-1917)

Antoine's younger brother and playmate, they often quarrelled and reconciled immediately. They talked about engines, airplanes and railways. He was very gifted for mathematics and music, he studied the cello. He was, with Antoine, a student at the Sainte-Croix college in Le Mans, then intern in Saint-Jean in Friborg. François, aged 15 died of rheumatic fever contracted while both were attending the college in Fribourg, Switzerland. Saint-Exupéry attended to his brother, his closest confidant, beside François' death bed, and later wrote that François '...remained motionless for an instant. He did not cry out. He fell as gently as a young tree falls', imagery which would much later be recrafted into the climactic ending of The Little Prince. Francois drew up a will, leaving his bicycle and a rifle to his brother.

Gabrielle de Saint-Exupery (1903-1986)

The only one of Antoine's sibblings to have children. Born May 15, 1903 in Lyon, the last daughter of Jean and Marie de Saint-Exupéry received the name of Gabrielle in tribute to her aunt, Mme de Tricaud. On October 11, 1923, Gabrielle married at the Château de Saint-Maurice Pierre de Giraud d'Agay whose parents were friends of the Fonscolombe family. Their neighbors, owned orchards and vineyards. Born on December 13, 1900 in Saint-Raphaël, Pierre, who made the Beauvais Agricultural Institute and the Aix School of Agriculture, ran the family farm in Saint-Raphaël. After the loss of a first child, Gabrielle d'Agay had four more. Antoine was the godfather of François, born in 1925. Affectionate with his nephews and nieces, Antoine de Saint-Exupéry built a privileged relationship with his godson who he often saw during his regular visits to Saint-Raphaël. Gabrielle d'Agay died on August 4, 1986 in Fréjus and Pierre on April 14, 1996 in Saint-Raphaël.

As of 2019 the two remaining living decendants, sons of Gabrielle, nephews of Antoine were
Francois de Giraud D'Agay and Jean de Giroaud D'Agay.

Marie Madeleine de Saint Exupery (1897-1927)

Caroline Fernande Marie-Madeleine, the oldest daughter of Jean and Marie de Saint Exupéry, was born on January 26, 1897 in Lyon. Of a fragile constitution, she was a shy and reserved child. She was the favorite of Aunt Tricaud and nicknamed 'Biche' by her maternal grandfather Charles de Fonscolombe, and also 'Mimma' by her brothers and sisters. She was the author of a collection of short stories entitled Les Amis de Biche which expressed her attachment to nature and animals. Suffering from tuberculosis, she died on June 2, 1927 at the Château de Saint-Maurice-de-Rémens.

Simone de Saint Exupery (1898-1978)

Gabrielle Charlotte Marie Simone de Saint-Exupéry was born in 1898 in Lyon, January 26, the same day as her older sister Marie-Madeleine. She was nicknamed "Monot" by her brothers and sisters. She studied Charters and wrote a thesis in 1928 entitled: History of the Benedictine Abbey of Ambronay, from the origins to the Revolution. She then worked as a paleographer in France and Indochina where she was for twenty years curator at the Archives and Libraries of French Indochina. Under the pseudonym Simone de Remens, she published in 1943 a volume of short proses: Meteors and published The lieutenant, the lady and the monkey. She was also the author of a volume of memories entitled: Five children in a park, published by Gallimard editions twenty years after his death.

Meeting The Little Prince

France

Lyon, France

I knew there was a statue of the statue of Antoine de Saint-Exupéry, author of my favourite book 'The Little Prince' somewhere outside the airport, also named after him. This was the reason for my visit, to visit the airport named after him. For most, hardly one of the wonders of the world, but for me, the dream of a lifetime. Finally outside the airport train station I found it. I felt no shame or embarrassment in asking a passer-by to take my photograph. The airport was originally named Lyon Satolas Airport, but in 2000 the airport and train station were renamed in honour of Lyonnais aviation pioneer and writer Antoine de Saint-Exupéry, on the centenary of his birth. The monumental bronze, high of 3,20 m (about 125 inches height), was installed on the forecourt of the TGV station in the airport complex of Lyon-Saint-Exupéry, connecting point of Lyon-Metropole and Region Auvergne Rhône-Alpes county with the world. Supported by the Saint-Exupery Succession and hosted by SNCF, the monument was given to the Community of Communes of East Lyon. The project, carried by the Foundation Lea and Napoleon Bullukian, was funded through patronage. The first donations from private individuals and companies have already helped producing the template in resin, at scale one, of the sculpture. It was officially inaugurated October 11th , 2017.

La Place Bellecour is a large square in the centre of Lyon to the north of the Ainay district. Measuring 15 acres it is one of the largest open squares without any patches of greenery or trees in Europe, and the third biggest square in France. It is also the largest pedestrian square in Europe. In the middle is an equestrian statue of King Louis XIV. Another statue, representing the Little Prince and Antoine de Saint Exupery sits at the west end of the square. The square also has two pavilions, housing the tourist information office of Lyon and an art gallery. At the far west end of the square is the monument dedicated to Saint-Exupéry which consists of a marble column on which the writer sits. Behind him, the Little Prince leans on his shoulder. The monument measures 5.50m and weighs 7 tonnes. Three sentences extracted from his work are engraved in marble:
'I will appear to be dead and it will not be true'.
'A star was shining and I was already contemplating it'.
'We only see well with the heart, the essential is 'invisible to the eyes'.

Created on the initiative of Frank Béjat, this monument was offered to the city of Lyon on June 29, 2000 by the Saint-Ex 2000 Committee. For the centenary of the birth of Antoine de Saint-Exupéry, the city of Lyon organized, on June 29, 2000, a major event in Place Bellecour. During this ceremony, a statue in honor of the writer was unveiled in the square. It is the work of a Lyon artist Christiane Guillaubey.

The pride that Lyon has for this celebrated writer and pilot is reflected not only in this statue but also in the street which bears his name. And why is Rue Saint-Exupéry located to one side of Bellecour square? Well, house number 8 of said street is precisely where the author was born. On this building there is a plaque commemorating this fact. Although the house where Antoine de Saint-Exupéry was born is in Lyon, there's no access to the general public. However, his childhood home, in another of the Rhône-Alpes region, is now a museum dedicated to his life and work. So, although you can't go to a museum in Lyon, you can walk along Rue Saint-Exupéry, look at the statue and then spend some time in the gardens next to Bellecour Square.

Famous People from Lyon wall painting, Lyon, France

Corner 49 Quai St Vincent and 2 rue de la Martinière - 69001 Lyon
The part adjoining Rue Martinière (600m2): Level 2: The Little Prince and Antoine de St-Exupéry.

This mural (covering 800m²) represents 2000 years of history with 25 historical Lyonnais figures and 6 contemporary. It was created by the Cité de la Création in 1994/1995.

La Fresque des Lyonnais, or the Mural of Lyonnais, is a building mural covering the back and side of a bright yellow building on the Saône side of the 1st arrondissement. It is one of the most popular historical monuments for city tourists, depicting some of the many Lyonnais who made the city what it is. It consists of 25 historic and six contemporary figures, with the modern-day characters painted at street-level to represent them interacting amongst today's residents and visitors. The nine-month project took this windowless, characterless wall in the city center and turned it into a veritable destination of Lyonnais culture. It was painted by the artist cooperative between 1994 to 1995 in an effort to revitalize the central intersection of one of Lyon's most central and heavily-trafficked districts.

The Little Prince Park, Ungersheim, France

Little Prince Park F- 68190 Ungersheim
15 km from Mulhouse train station and 4 km from Bollwiller train station
40 km from Euroairport Basel-Mulhouse.

1 Day Adult (above 12 years)	21,00 €
1 Day Child (+1 m to 11years)	17,00 €
1 Day Family Avalaible for 4 persons	69,00 €

The park is difficult to get to but a free bus from Lille railway station helps those without a car.

The Little Prince Park opened its doors on July 1st, 2014 in Ungersheim in the heart of Alsace. An original ‚A ‚French twist and unique concept of a theme park it ranks as the first aerial park in the world. On more than 24 hectares, the Little Prince Park invites its visitors to a poetic trip on the planet of Saint-Exupéry's hero The Little Prince and promises over thirty attractions and shows divided into three major themes, The Flight : Two giant tethered balloons, the Aerobar, the Wave Swinger, the Aerousel. The planet to planet Trip : 3D and 4D movie theaters; and The Animals : foxes, sheep, acrobatic pigeons, gardens and butterfly greenhouses, a rose garden and the labyrinth of the Fountain .

From The Little Prince's Park, 'In the heart of Alsace, between Colmar and Mulhouse, come and live with your family, an unforgettable experience in the world's first air park! "All adults have once been children but few of them remember" In one day, find your child's soul with 34 attractions and new events that will immerse you in the poetic universe of the Little Prince Antoine de Saint-Exupéry.

The Little Prince Park isn't just an amusement park with fun and fast rides, it takes an educational stance through fun. Dotted around the park were numerous swings and see-saws. A little train took the visitors around the park stopping at various attractions. There were the normal amusement park rides like the log flume and carousel. Two huge hot air balloons, The Kings and The Lamplighters, gave an interactive ride high above the park. There were two theaters showing short films, some in 3D, in various languages. At 'Draw me a sheep', a huge blackboard where visitors could use the chalk provided to draw a sheep or The Little Prince for themselves. Walk through the maze and into the rose garden where a statue of a rose in a glass case stands. Indoors, the exhibition of the author Saint Exupery, a history of his life as a pilot and author, and the underwater planet 4D attraction.

There is the petting zoo, housing sheep, rabbits, chickens, peacocks and miniature goats. Other activities include The Trampoline Park and The flying chairs. Finally spend your last hour in the gift shop. Like a child in a sweet shop with everything, from toys to table ware, clothing to collectibles, posters to writing pads, pens and pencils.

National Air and Space Museum, Paris, France

The Air and Space Museum at Paris's Le Bourget Airport in cooperation with The Estate of Saint-Exupéry-d'Agay, have created a permanent exhibit of 300 m² dedicated to the author, pilot, person and humanist. The Espace Saint-Exupéry exhibit, officially inaugurated in 2006 on the anniversary of the aviator's birthday, traces each stage of his life as an airmail pioneer, eclectic intellectual-artist and military pilot. It includes artifacts from his life: photographs, his drawings, letters, some of his original notebooks he scribbled in voluminously and which were later published posthumously, plus remnants of the unarmed P-38 he flew on his last reconnaissance mission and which were recovered from the Mediterranean Sea.

Opening hours of the Air and Space Museum
The museum is open all week except on Mondays, from 10 a.m. to 5 p.m.
Fees of special collections and activities at the Air Museum. Permanent collections are free or those under 26 years of age, but visits aircraft, pilot planet, are subject to a charge.
How to get to the Air Museum?
RER line B stop: Le Bourget, then take bus 152

National Homage To Antoine de Saint-Exupéry at the Pantheon

Panthéon Place du Panthéon, 75005 Paris
By subway / RER line 10 / RER B By bus lines 21, 27, 38, 82, 84, 85, 89
Entry Adult 11.5€

Saint-Exupéry is commemorated with an inscription in the

Pantheon in Paris, France's repository of historical greats. Although his body was never identified, his name was added to the Panthéon in November 1967 by a French legislative act. The inscription reads: A la memoire de Antoine de Saint-Exupéry poete romancier aviateur disparu au cours d'une mission de reconnaissance aerienne le 31 juillet 1944' (To the memory of Antoine de Saint Exupery, poet, novelist, aviator, missing during an aerial reconnaissance mission, 31 July 1944). Amongst other honours from France, he was named a Chevalier de la Legion d'honneur in April 1930 and was promoted to an Officier de la Légion d'honneur in January 1939. He was awarded the Croix de guerre in 1940 and was posthumously awarded the Croix de guerre avec Palme in 1944.

Le Petit Prince Store, Paris, France
8 rue Grégoire de Tours 75006, Paris

She re-blossomed last spring, leaving boulevard Arago behind for rue Grégoire-de-Tours, in Saint-Germain-des-Prés. Although the store may not quite be the small prince's rose, she's close: the boutique store is entirely dedicated to this recognisable character from the children's book. Thomas Rivière, the great nephew of Antoine de Saint-Exupéry, is the shop's owner, and you might say that by moving the little Prince Store into one of these more touristy areas, the owner is playing more of a commercial game. Translated into more than 260 languages, The Little Prince is read by hundreds of millions of readers across the world, and there are many potential buyers. If you need convincing, take a look at the library bookshelf, which is generally flooded with differing dialects of this popular tale.

But the Little Prince products don't stop with just books. Pens, notebooks, snowglobes, mugs and dolls. There are no limits to marketing on the back of this little hero. Ironic, given the book itself denounces exacerbated materialism in our society.

National School of Fine Arts, Paris, France
14 Rue Bonaparte, 75006 Paris, France

Whilst not pursuing it as a career, the well-known pilot and writer Antoine de Saint-Exupéry studied architecture here.

Quai Saint-Exupéry, Seine, Paris, France

The Quai Saint-Exupery is a dock located along the Seine in Paris in the 16th District.
Starting at Boulevard Morat and ending at Boulogne Billancourt. It is 630m long. Dedicated in 1976.

Le Petit Prince de Paris Restaurant Paris
rue de Lanneau 75005 - PARIS ue de l'industrie

Located in the historic Latin Quarter, close to the Pantheon and the site of the old Gallo-Roman baths, 'Le Petit Prince de Paris' was an old tavern in 1450, popular throughout the ages by famous people as François Villon, the most famous poet of the late Middle Ages. Transformed into a mansion, he became in 1976 the iconic restaurant Tout Paris.

Buste d'Antoine de Saint-Exupéry
1 avenue de la Motte Picquet Square Santiago de Chile, 75007 Paris, France.

A bust of Saint-Exupéry by sculpture Madeleine de Tazenas.

Plaque Saint-Exupéry, Place Vauban, Paris
15 place Vauban in Paris I

Plaque opposite Avenue de Tourville of the pilot who lived there 1934 to 1940.

Père Lachaise Cemetery, Paris, France
Face au 21 boulevard de Ménilmontant - 75020 Paris

The Père Lachaise cemetery takes its name from King Louis XIV's confessor, Father François d'Aix de La Chaise. It is the most prestigious and most visited necropolis in Paris. Situated in the 20th arrondissement of Paris, it extends 44 hectares and contains 70,000 burial plots. The cemetery is a mix between an English park and a shrine. All funerary art styles are represented: Gothic graves, Haussmanian burial chambers, ancient mausoleums, etc. On the green paths, visitors cross the burial places of famous men and women; Honoré de Balzac, Guillaume Apollinaire, Frédéric Chopin, Colette, Jean-François Champollion, Jean de La Fontaine, Molière, Yves Montand, Simone Signoret, Jim Morrison, Alfred de Musset, Edith Piaf, Camille Pissarro and Oscar Wilde are just a few.

Independent tour: Free admission for all visitors. Guided tour: Saturdays and Sundays. Free
Consuelo de Saint- Exupéry a Salvadoran-French writer and artist, and wife of the writer and aviator Antoine de Saint Exupéry is buried in the "89éme Division" of the cemetery. Best is to enter through Porte Gambetta, not far from Métro Gambetta, and turn immediately left as you enter, it will then be the second section or block on your right. Other interesting celebrities in that section are Georges Courteline and Oscar Wilde. Her tomb is next to her first husband's, Enrique Gomez

Carillo.

Heureux Comme Alexandre, Orleans, France
52 rue Sainte Catherine, 45000, Orleans, France

A small restaurant with a concept of 3 signature dishes, which can be prepared at the table by the guests, and the theme of Saint-Exupéry's Little Prince.
Distance from Paris 75 miles, 1 Hour by train

Little Prince Stone carving, Palavas-les-Flots, France
2 Rue Pierre de Provence, 34250 Palavas-les-Flots, France

Stone statue of Saint-Exupéry holding the hand of The Little Prince at a roundabout in the town.
Distance from Paris 475 miles, Montpellier 9 miles

Little Prince and Fox statues, Amberieu-en-Bugey, France
Aérodrome Amberieux en Bugey

Stéphane Paret, sculptor from Rambert, produced the work that sits on the new roundabout at the motorway exit. This represents Antoine de Saint-Exupéry, whose gaze is turned towards the airfield of Ambérieu. It's hard to count how many congratulatory messages Stéphane Paret has received. When the roundabout at the Chateau-Gaillard highway entrance was inaugurated in June 2012.Elected officials and volunteers of the Souvenir de Saint-Exupéry association had nothing but praise for him. 'I am happy with this achievement, but not proud. Otherwise, we can no longer advance', soberly slips the sculptor.

Distance from Paris 300 miles, Lyon 35 miles

Saint-Exupéry Cabris

Figurines of The Little Prince (Le Petit Prince) can be seen everywhere in Cabris, recalling that the Countess de Saint-Exupéry, mother of the writer and pioneering pilot, lived here for 40 years, between 1934 and 1971. Murals and placards erected in 1994 on the walls of his mothers home.
Distance from Paris 480 miles, Marseille 11 miles

Le Petit Restaurant, Cabris, France
15 Rue Frederic Mistral, 06530 Cabris

At the heart of Cabris, perched village in the sky of the French Riviera (550 m), 10 min. Grasse, perfume capital, the Little Prince's team welcomes you in a warm and rustic setting. The terrace opens onto the country setting with trees 'Petit Pré' Cabris. The room, with exposed beams and stone, is decorated with illustrations of The Little Prince: Countess Marie de Saint Exupéry, who lived in Cabris from 1934 to 1971, agreed in the sixties that this restaurant is named after the book.
Distance from Nice 35km

Saint-Exupéry Statue Toulouse, France

Royal Garden, Toulouse, 31000, France

For the hundredth anniversary of the birth of Saint-Exupéry, the City of Toulouse ordered a statue. It was erected at the Royal Garden in fall 2000. The bronze statue of the writer within his hand a book with the figure of the Little Prince. The

statue stands in a bronze globe, and measures 3 x 1.5m.
Tezenas du Montcel, French sculptor.
Distance from Paris 421 miles

The Triple Life of Avenue Saint-Exupéry, Toulouse, France

Avenue Saint-Exupéry in Toulouse leads to Montaudran where the Aeropostale aerodrome and the Latécoère workshops were located. A fresco (3mx10m) with his effigy was drawn there in 2010.

Eccentric, away from line A of the metro, far from the future line B, avenue Saint-Exupéry displays an insolent good humor. This long artery which unites the bourgeois residences of the Pont des Demoiselles with the opulent but already almost rural place de l'Ormeau, is the last of the six main streets which, from the Faubourg Bonnefoy, form a district, descending the city from east to west to the Canal du Midi. Simply named Route de Revel until 1955, avenue Saint-Exupéry did not just bear the name of the famous aviator. Immersed in the history of transport, it oscillates between the memory of the barges which dropped in dry dock in the refit basin located just across the Pont des Demoiselles, and the still close presence of aviation pioneers. The garage is the old Plenacoste bicycle garage. This is where Didier Daurat and Antoine de Saint-Exupéry handed over their bicycles before walking to Montaudran airport to join their planes.

The avenue with its 80 shops retains its vitality. For the inhabitants, there is not one, but three Saint-Exupéry avenues. The first one which runs from the Pont des Demoiselles to the railway bridge, concentrates the shops, sometimes luxurious, frequented by the wealthy occupants of Toulouse and small buildings comfortably installed in the network of adjacent residential streets. Then comes an intermediate section where trade becomes scarce as one moves away from the railway bridge towards the Courrège gendarmerie barracks. Finally, from the barracks to the Place de l'Ormeau, the avenue loses almost all of its stores, and the habitat takes comfort in the middle of spacious gardens. The abundance of signs and shops that flourish between the bridges is only a vague memory. Saint-Exupéry is about to merge with its almost twin sister, the very select avenue Jean-Rieux.

Langley Hotel, Le Petit Prince, Alpe D'Huez, France
Rue de la Poste, 38750 Alpe d'Huez, Rhône-Alpes

Langley Hotel le Petit Prince is a charming hotel, located in Alpe d'Huez. The closest lift is just around the corner, and the city center is no further than a five minute walk. With approximately 300 days of sun and a stunning view of the valley below, this is the place to visit if you are looking for a relaxing family holiday. With its extraordinary views from the bar and restaurant, Le Petit Prince is the perfect place to hang out after a day in the slopes. Gather friends and family for some board games next to our fireplace in the hotel lounge. Distance from Paris 400 miles, Lyon 104 miles

Huge Copy of Little Prince Book, Aix-en-Provence, France
8-10 rue des Allumettes, Aix-en-Provence, 13100, France

If any passersby were curious what awaited them inside the Bibliotheque Mejanes, the three colossal books that make up the library's facade should help take some of the mystery out of

it.
The Bibliotheque Mejanes was originally founded in 1810 and was located in the town hall of the provincial city of Aix. Since 1989 it has formed part of the Cite du Livre complex built into a former match factory. Incorporating a number of research institutes, as well as fulfilling the function of a public library, its most striking aspect is its architectural frontage, which takes the form of three giant-sized books: Albert Camus's L'Etranger (The Outsider/The Stranger), Antoine de Saint-Exupery's Little Prince, and the writings of Moliere. There may be no library in the world that caters to BIG readers quite so directly.
Distance from Paris 475 miles, Marseille 20 miles

L'école Le Petit Prince, Grenech, France

A public elementary school in the small community of Genech in northern France, dedicated in 1994 upon the merger of two former schools. With nine classrooms and a library, its building overlooks the village's Place Terre des Hommes a square also named in tribute to Saint-Exupéry's 1939 philosophical memoir.
Distance from Paris 148 miles

The Little Prince Crèche, Marseille, France
8 Rue borde perpendiculaire - 13008 Marseille

A 680m2 nursery with 58 cradles including the exteriors.

Castle Saint-Exupéry Saint-Maurice-de-Rémens, France
548 rue de la liberation, Saint-Maurice-de-Rémens, France

The castle of Saint-Maurice-de-Rémens is a castle in Saint-Maurice-de-Remens. It is sometimes nicknamed Château du Petit Prince or Château de Saint-Ex because of the link between the building and Antoine de Saint-Exupéry. The author lived in what was family property during much of his childhood. As he said himself, he spent 'the best moments of his life there'. Whether in his personal correspondence or in his books, Saint-Exupéry regularly refers to Saint-Maurice. In September 2018 saw the inauguration of the "Liberty Bench" dedicated to the writer at the entrance of the castle

The Auvergne-Rhône-Alpes region announced in September 2019 the acquisition of Antoine de Saint-Exupéry's castle in the small town of Saint-Maurice-de-Remens (Ain), to create a museum that could well become a tourist hotspot. On site, the development work could last two years, with a budget between 25 and 30 million euros. In Japan, there is a replica of the castle of Saint-Exupéry, in the city of Hakoné. Japanese tourists flock to discover the atmosphere of the Little Prince. The castle museum of Saint-Exupéry could well attract crowds.

Antoine's parents were married at Saint-Maurice. His father Jean and his only brother Francois were buried there. Distance from Paris 290 miles, Lyon 34 miles

Notre Dame de Mongré High School, Villefranche-sur-Saône, France

276 Avenue Saint-Exupéry, 69652 Villefranche-sur-Saône, France

A private and catholic school in Villefranche-sur-Saône, Rhone, France. The school was founded in 1848 as a Jesuit institution. Mongré currently enrolls just over 2,000 students from elementary school to high school and is proud to achieve

high grades and results for the baccalaureat.
Distance from Paris 271 miles, Lyon 20 miles

The Tomb Of Antoine de Saint-Exupery, Carqueiranne, France (Desputed)

17-145 Chemin du Petit Lac, 83320 Carqueiranne, France

Saint-Exupéry Antoine (de) (1900-1944), writer and aviator. Disappeared in flight, off Marseille. In the Carqueiranne cemetery, an anonymous tomb shelters the remains of a man whose body wearing a French uniform was found by a fisherman in 1944. No exhumation has been carried out to date to verify the remains.
Distance from Paris 530 miles, Marseille 48 miles

Fountain Saint-Exupéry Chateau D'Agay, Agay, France

1510, boulevard de la Baumette, 83530 Agay

The great pilot and writer, Antoine de Saint-Exupéry stayed with his sister, Gabrielle d'Agay at château d'Agay. He got married there in 1932 with Consuelo Suncin and spent his last european Christmas there in 1940. A fountain dedicated to Le Petit Prince stands a few steps away from Résidence Agathos as a tribute to this immortal book, translated into more than 180 languages, and a plaque on Baumette Lighthouse pays tribute to this aviator who died for France on the 31st july 1944.
Distance from Paris 553 miles, Cannes 18 miles

Baumette Lighthouse, Agay, France

The Agay lighthouse, also known as Baumette lighthouse, is

located on the seaside resort of Agay, which belongs to the town of Saint-Raphaël, in the Var, at the foot of the Esterel mountains. The lighthouse was built in 1884, and has a square shape surmounting a main building. Top 17 m, it overcomes the sea level of nearly 30 m. Positioned on the tip of Baumettes which partly closes the harbor of Agay, its range is about 27 km.

A stele was built at its base in memory of the writer and aviator Antoine de Saint-Exupéry. On July 31, 1944, while joining his unit in Corsica the author of the Little Prince flew over the villa of his brother-in-law, Count d'Agay then the lighthouse, which would have been the last building seen by the pilot.
Distance from Paris 553 miles, Cannes 18 miles

Cultural Space Saint-Exupéry Franconville, France
32 Rue de la Station, 95130 Franconville, France

Built in the early 1990s by Francis Delattre and his team, Espace Saint-Exupéry, whose architecture was designed to match the shape of an airplane, brings together within its walls a theater and cinema hall of 423 seats, an exhibition hall, a multipurpose room, 2 e cinemas and a multimedia library. Many live performance events, exhibitions and autograph sessions are held throughout the year.

Espace Saint-Exupéry opening hours
Tuesday 8:30 a.m. to 12:30 p.m. and 1:30 p.m. to 7 p.m.
Wednesday, Thursday and Friday 8:30 a.m. to 12:30 p.m. and 1:30 p.m. to 6 p.m.
Saturday 8:30 a.m. to 6 p.m.
Distance from Paris 10 miles

Saint-Exupéry Cinema Marignane, France
53 Avenue Jean Mermoz, 13700 Marignane, France

Distance from Paris 474 miles, Marseilles 15 miles

The Star Saint-Exupéry Cinema, Strasbourg, France
18 Rue du Vingt-Deux Novembre, 67000 Strasbourg, France

Distance from Paris 304 miles, Nancy 97 miles

Europe

Le Petit Prince Patisserie, Bournemouth, England
48B Poole Road Westbourne, Bournemouth BH4 9DZ England

A small family independent French- style Bakery and Patisserie. All our bread and goods are made freshly every day on the premises. A range of quality breakfast, lunches, barista-style coffee and loose - brewed teas. Sandwiches are served on freshly baked whole grain and sourdough bread.

Le Petit Prince Bar, Zurich, Switzerland
Address Bleicherweg 21 | 8002 Zürich

After 30 years of exclusive clubbing in Zurich, Le Petit Prince club is reborn. A thorough renovation, a new management team, a premium DJ line up and music program as well as an international and beautiful crowd will bring the comeback of one of the oldest and finest venues in Zurich. Le Petit Prince stands for exclusiveness and genuine hospitality as we strive to provide an excellent service to our guests. Located at Bleicherweg 21 in Zurich's business district, just steps away from Paradeplatz and Bahnhofstrasse, you will find a place to dream. A small and unique location with its charming Parisian flair of glamour and elegance. Le Petit Prince opens its doors every night from Sunday to Sunday for only 150 individually selected members and guests. For the privacy of our celebrities we do not allow local media to enter and to take pictures. Furthermore, we offer VIP guests special services, such as a separate entrance.

Directions
Le Petit Prince is located just steps away from Paradeplatz and Bahnhofstrasse at Bleicherweg 21 in Zurich's business district.
Public Transit: Tramway number 6/7/8/13 (Station Stockerstrasse)

Villa St. Jean International School, Fribourg, Switzerland

Originally named Collège Villa St. Jean, was a private Catholic school in Fribourg, Switzerland from 1903 to 1970. Prior to its closure it was the final remaining all-boys' boarding school in Switzerland. Founded in Switzerland in 1903, during an upheaval of anti-clericalism in France, as a boarding school for the scions of the French elite, Villa St Jean International School evolved over the decades into an international school educating students from around the world. Deceased illustrious alumni include the aviator and author Antoine-de-Saint-Exupéry (who attended with his younger brother).

Despite their architectural and historical significance, most of the campus buildings were razed in 1981, a travesty which would not have been permitted under more recently enacted Swiss architectural preservation laws. Apart from a wooden-roofed outdoor basketball pavilion, the only building that was left standing, and which still stands today, is Gallia Hall, which served as the principal classroom and laboratory building. Distance from Zurich 98 miles

Hotel "Der Kleine Prinz" Baden-Baden · Germany

Lichtentaler Str. 36 · 76530 Baden-Baden · Germany

The charming hotel has over 40 elegant and individually decorated rooms and suites. You will find touching motives throughout the hotel that remind of Saint-Exupéry's story The Little Prince.

Restaurant Der Kleine Prinz, Baden-Baden, Germany

Lichtentaler Str. 36, 76530, Baden-Baden, Baden-Württemberg Germany

This family-run hotel-restaurant in the town centre of Baden Baden has the story of the Little Prince running right through it. The restaurant has fairy tale motifs, gilt-framed mirrors, an open fireplace and renaissance furniture. It serves seasonal French and Baden dishes for lunch and candlelit dinners. It also has a selection of dishes for vegetarians and diabetics.

Lycée Français Antoine-de-Saint-Exupéry de Hambourg, Germany

Hartsprung 23, 22529 Hamburg, Germany

It serves kindergarten through senior high school

Little Prince volcano sculpture, Heerlen, Netherlands

Kloosterkensweg, Heerlen 6419

Image of the Little Prince sweeping a volcano on his 'planet', with the rose in the background. On a missing information board it said (van HeerlenZien): The Little Prince is a book by Antoine de Saint-Exupéry. The little prince takes care of and

looks after his little planet. He cleans the volcanoes, frees his planet from dangerous monkey bread trees and protects the rose from cold and wind. He learns how to carry responsibility and derive pleasure and joy from it. Bonifatius Stirnberg (Freienohl 1933), German sculptor.
Distance from Amsterdam 134 miles, Eindhoven 54 miles

Le Petit Prince Culture Cafe, Lisbon, Portugal
Rua Cecilio de Sousa 1A, Lisbon 1200-098 Portugal

Café, gallery, second hand French library.

Little Prince Sculpture, Skopje, Macedonia
15, Dimitar Vlahov Walk 1000, Skopje 1000, North Macedonia

Youth Cultural Center (MKC) is a Skopje based cultural institution that organizes more than 200 different cultural events per year - performances, exhibitions, promotions, workshops, concerts, debates and film screenings. YCC also organizes four of the most important festivals in Macedonia. Large statue of The Little Prince standing on his planet at the entrance to the centre.

Little Prince Fountain, Round Garden, Tbilissi, Republic of Georgia
Lovel Kutateladze Street, Tbilissi

Some people say, that the Round Garden is kind of a border between Vera and Vake neighbourhoods. Such an tiny island between the rushy streets with trees and benches and bushes, and a couple of coffee houses near it. Mother with children obviously like it not least because of the fountain with the Little Prince. Round Garden is also a good spot to take a break during Vera-Vake exploring, and to look what Vakeli people actually are, if you are into urban anthropology.

Little Prince Apartments , Corfu, Greece
Agios Stefanos Greece

'This was our third visit to the Little Prince and it really did feel like we were coming home we had a lovely welcome from Michael an Anna we were delighted with our room which was big modern and spotlessly clean lovely pool and snack bar great restaurant and the cocktail bar fantastic all the staff work hard to ensure you have a great time.san Stefanos itself is a lovely resort lots of great bars and restaurants'.

Riells Beach l'Escala, Costa Brava, Spain

It has been a few years since the village of l'Escala has become the place where the Little Prince, the character of Antoine de Saint-Exupéry's novel, decided to stay and live. On Riells beach, in l'Escala, the Little Prince contemplates sitting on a stone wall, every evening, the sunset of the Costa Brava. Many visitors are surprised by its figure, next to which they are photographed, and also by the fox, which is a few meters along the promenade from the same beach. Later on the boulevard (which bears the Catalan name of the character:Petit Príncep) you will also find references to the novel, such as because there is one on the ground a rose, baobab, palms which draw constellations of the East and volcanic rocks.

Saint Exupéry School, Madrid, Spain
Calle del Camino Ancho, 85, 28109 Alcobendas, Madrid, Spain

French Educational school

El Petit Princep Restaurant, Barcelona, Spain
Gran Via de les Cortes Catalanes 677, 08013 Barcelona Spain

Ecologic and superfoods ingridients, vegan options, specialty coffee, home made, kombucha, microlots teas, fresh juices, craft Barcelonas beer surrounded by Little Prince artwork.

The Little Prince Statue, Zagreb, Croatia

This cute statue of The Little Prince statue is located in Borongaj neighborhood in Zagreb, Croatia. The author of this statue is Nada Orel and it was created in 1985. Bronze statue of the Little Prince sweeping one of his vulcanos on his astroid B 612. On the side is the mysterious rose that began growing on the asteroid's surface. In addition to this bronze figure there are five carved stone blocks with scenes from the story. The blocks are connected by stone paths. The planet with the lamplighter, inscription: Dobro veče - Dobro jutro / Good evening - good morning.

North America

Little Prince Restaurant New York
199 Prince Street, Soho, New York

Little Prince is located at 199 Prince Street in SoHo (between Sullivan St. and MacDougal St.) We aim to be a cozy neighborhood stand-by. Little Prince features classic French bistro items. Dramatic floral arrangements accent the light-filled space, which has floor-to-ceiling windows that look out on bustling Prince Street. Caramel banquettes line the walls and the wooden bar is warmly lit by classic globe pendant lamps. Hand-painted ceramic floor tiles complete the bistro ambience.

Bevin Mansion, Asharoken, Long Island
76 Bevin Rd, Northport, NY 11768, United States

The elegant victorian Bevin House sits on a point jutting into Northport Bay, on the peninsular village of Asharoken, Long Island. It's here, staring into Duck Island Harbor, that author Antoine de Saint-Exupéry wrote the majority of his classic novella, Le Petit Prince during the summer of 1942.
The Bevin House is a Victorian mansion located at 76 Bevin Road in the village of Asharoken in northern Long Island near New York. This is where, during late 1942, Antoine de Saint-Exupery wrote The Little Prince in less then two months. The house had been rented by Consuelo, Saint-Exupery's wife. For a while it was the couple's 'house of happiness'. They entertained many friends there and among them were Andre Maurois and the Swiss philosopher Denis de Rougemont with whom Saint-Exupery played endless games of chess. The

house was built in 1862 by Cornelius Henry DeLamater and remained property of the family, which became Bevin by marriage, until 1960. In 1964 it was sold to Charles William Foesell. In 1979 the estate was purchased by real estate developer Nikos Kefalidis who commissioned an extensive restoration of the mansion. Kefalidis was unfortunately killed in the crash of Swissair flight SR 111 on 2 September 1998.

The Bevin House is still owned today by the Kefalidis family. Unfortunately it cannot be visited.
Distance from Central Park 45 miles

The Little Prince Statue, Northport, New York
151 Laurel Avenue, Northport, New York, United States

The town library has honored this local literary figure with a statue of the Little Prince. The piece is cast in bronze, a three-foot, three-dimensional likeness of the character. It sits in the library's courtyard, and is the only version of the statue in existence, the molds having been intentionally destroyed after casting in order to ensure this Little Prince remains a one-of-a-kind.

The beloved character ended up welcoming visitors to the library through the efforts of another French expatriate, a Northport local named Yvette Cariou O'Brien. O'Brien worked tirelessly with the de Saint-Exupéry estate to secure permission to create the work, and in 2006 it was unveiled.
Antoine de Saint-Exupéry ended up in Northport having left occupied France after its fall to German forces at the start of World War II. Although he lived in Manhattan, the noise and heat of a New York City summer wasn't exactly encouraging for the writer and his poignant, philosophical creation. That's what houses by the sea and good libraries are for.

Know Before You Go
Located at the Northport-East Northport Public Library. Library parking (a very small lot) is located off Scudder Avenue. You can enter from the front or the rear. There is a stairwell across from the circulation desk; go down the stairs and into the courtyard straight ahead. As you enter the courtyard, the Little Prince is on your left.
Library Hours

9:00 a.m. -9:00 p.m. Monday - Friday 9:00 a.m. -5:00 p.m. Saturday
1:00 p.m. -5:00 p.m. Sunday (mid September through mid June)
Train approx 2 hours from Central Park, NY City.

Commemorative plaque Saint-Exupéry New York
La Vie Parisienne (3 East 52nd St.)

On the exterior of the second floor of a Midtown building rests a plaque commemorating Saint-Exupéry. In French and English, the plaque says several chapters of The Little Prince were written in a studio at 3 East 52nd St. The studio actually was being used by Bernard Lamotte, a Parisian painter. It is said that his circle of artistic friends included luminaries such as actor-sketch writer Charlie Chaplin, actor-singer Marlene Dietrich, and of course, Saint-Exupéry. On the ground floor of the building was La Vie Parisienne (The Parisian Life), a French restaurant. Today, patrons can take in fine French dining at the same location courtesy of the restaurant La Grenouille (The Frog). The plaque is reportedly below where Lamotte's table sat. Installed October 2000.

Saint-Exupéry's residence, Central Park, New York
240 Central Park South

Saint-Exupéry actually lived in three locations in the New York City area. Less than 20 minutes' walk from La Vie Parisienne, Saint-Exupéry would have found the location an easy stroll from where he gathered with his friends. Just across the road from the six-decade-old building is Columbus Circle and Central Park itself, providing a respite from New York City's busy streets if Saint-Exupéry desired it. When Saint-Exupéry moved into the building in 1941, it was only a year old and considered to be very modern. Today, the two-tower building still looks very fresh courtesy of a renovation to its exterior a decade ago that among other things, restored the yellow-orange bricks to their former glory. The Souvenir Français society (which honours members of the French military) initially wanted to place the plaque at this location. The owner denied them because he feared it would bring in tourists.

Little Prince Restaurant, Santa Monica, California, USA
2424 Main St, Santa Monica, CA 90405-3516

Chef-driven farm-to-table shared plates, seasonal craft cocktails, and eclectic natural wines in a stylistic and vibrant neighborhood setting.

Cafe Saint-Ex, Washington, DC 20009 USA
corner of 14th & T Streets, 1847 14th Street NW, Washington, DC 20009

Nicknamed Gate 54, the downstairs bar at Cafe Saint-Ex offers a more casual atmosphere than the main dining room. The full dinner menu is available with first- come, first- serve seating. Gate 54 is the perfect space for a relaxed meal with friends, to hear your favorite DJ spinning, catch a comedy show,or host your next private event.

L'école élémentaire catholique Le Petit Prince. Maple, Ontario, Canada
Avro Road, Maple, Ontario

Opened in 1994 as L'école élémentaire catholique Le Petit Prince. Its enrollment expanded from 30 students in its first year to some 325 children by 2014. One of Saint-Exupéry's colourful paintings of the prince is found on its website's welcome page.

Quebec Home Plaque
25 Avenue Sainte-Geneviève, Québec, Qc Canada G1R4B1

Plate text
The people of Quebec remember
Here stayed in 1942, in the De Koninck family, Antoine de Saint-Exupéry (1900-1944) Author of The Little Prince
1999 (Installation of the commemorative property)

Charles De Koninck House, Old Quebec, Canada
25 rue Sainte-Geneviève,Quebec City, Canada

The large house of Charles de Koninck where Saint-Exupéry visited in 1942 and played with de Koninck's 8 year old son.

Antoine de Saint-Exupéry Secondary School, Montreal, Canada

5150 Boulevard Robert, Saint-Léonard, QC H1R 1P9, Canada

French language public secondary school.

South America

Antoine de Saint-Exupéry Airport, San Antonio Oeste, Argentina

Airport serving San Antonio Oeste, a city in the Rio Negro Province of Argentina. The airport is named after the French author-aviator Antoine de Saint-Exupéry. San Antonio Oeste's airport was renamed after the French writer-aviator Antoine de Saint-Exupéry, who frequently surveyed routes in the country as the director of Aeroposta Argentina, the company that created a stopover airport at that location en route to Comodoro Rivadavia. A small museum exhibit was created in the airport's terminal building honoring its origins. It came into being on October 31, 1929 when a flight route began between Comodoro Rivadavia and Bahia Blanca with stops at San Antonio Oeste. The following day Aeroposta Argentina inaugurated its regular service to the airport. Due to a lack of facility, runway, and airport maintenance for over 20 years, commercial air services were discontinued to the airport in 2009. Currently only the local flying club and some private flights use the facility.

Galería Güemes, Buenos Aires, Argentina
Florida Street 165, C1005 CABA, Argentina

The 16-story Galería Güemes, built in 1915, was the city's first skyscraper, and its top-floor mirador offers great downtown vistas. This restored galleria shines as a spectacular example of art nouveau architecture, complete with glass-domed ceilings, ornate metalwork, and gilt sculptural details. Not surprisingly, legend surrounds the building, including that in 1931, the writer of The Little Prince, Antoine de Saint-Exupéry, once lived in an upstairs apartment with a pet seal cub.

Galería Güemes, located in downtown Buenos Aires, is an architectural and cultural landmark: Antoine de Saint-Exupéry lived in the building for two years. The view from the top is just as notable. Take the elevator to the highest floor to access the mirador, or lookout, accessible by a tall spiral staircase. The attendant will provide you with a map of the view, which includes several notable buildings as well as a rare and sweeping view of the Rio de la Plata: on a clear day, you can see Uruguay across the water.

The Aguja Saint-Exupéry, Los Glaciares National Park Patagonia, Argentina

The Aguja Saint-Exupéry is a mountain spear ('aguja') located near the Cerro Chalte in the Los Glaciers National Park. The mountain is named in memory of Antoine de Saint Exupéry, who was director of the Aeroposta Argentina and pioneered postal flights in the Patagonia region between 1929 and 1931. The Aguja Saint-Exupéry is not as impressive as its taller neighbors Cerro Chaltén and the striking Cerro Torre but due to the length of its climbing routes and the extreme weather conditions of the southern Andes, it shares the same big wall reputation as most Patagonian peaks. It was first climbed on February 23, 1968.
Distance from Buenos Aires, 5 hour flight

Castillo San Carlos, San Carlos, Concordia, Argentina

Av. Belgrano y Mario Munoz Parque San Carlos, Concordia Argentina

This castle was built by the Demachy family by the end of 1880s. However, out of the sudden, they disappeared. After several auctions, many different families rented this large house. One particular family, the Fuchs Valon, of French origins, were living right there at the moment Antoine de Saint-Exupéry's plane obliged him to land there due to technical issues. It is said that some episodes from The Little Prince are based on the experiences Antoine went through while staying there.

The Place itself is really well-preserved and the view to the Uruguay River is outstanding. The green areas are perfect to enjoy having a picnic. There is a guided tour where the history of the families who used to lived there are told. On the basement, there is a pretty small museum documenting information about the castle and his visit.
Distance from Buenos Aires 270 miles

Little Prince Avenue, Campeche, Florianopolis, Brazil

The main avenue in the Campeche neighborhood, in Florianópolis, Avenida Pequeno Princípe route is a reference to the famous work of the French writer, illustrator and aviator Antoine de Saint-Exupéry. According to residents and researchers in Brazil and France, there are historical records of the writer's passage through the region, in the first part of the 20th century, more precisely between the years 1920 to 1940.

At that time, there was in the region of the Campeche district an aviation field used as a stopping point for pilots of the French post, the Latécoere, later called Aéro Postale. The company had Florianopolis on the mail delivery route between

Paris and Buenos Aires, Argentina. The aviation field was occasionally replaced by the current Florianópolis Airport. One of these pilots was Antoine de Saint-Exupéry and there are records of his presence in at least three passages around the place. The illustrious visitor and his several meetings with local fishermen, created a character of the local culture, originating the name of the avenue in honor of his most famous book: The Little Prince.
Distance from Rio de Janeiro 720 miles

Saint-Exupéry Airport, Ocauçu, São Paulo, Brazil

Saint-Exupéry Airport, Brazil, ICAO identifier SDDK, a small community airdrome in Ocauçu, São Paulo, Brazil

Bathtub artwork of the Little Prince, Havana, Cuba
Callejon de Hamel, Havan, Cuba

Callejon de Hamel is a narrow alley in Havana filled with lively colorful murals and sculptures made from bathtubs, hand pumps, and pinwheels. It offers visitors to Cuba's capital a taste of the city's local art. Cuban artist Salvador Gonzáles Escalona describes his Afro-Cuban style as a mix of surrealism, cubism, and abstract art. After spending more than two decades producing artworks in Cuba, as well as the U.S., Norway, Italy, and Venezuela, the self-taught artist began adorning the alley outside his apartment with art in 1990.

Little Prince Children's Playground, Cabrera, Mexico City, Mexico
Plaza Luis Cabrera

After El Péndulo, keep going to Calle Orizaba, at which point you need to turn left towards Plaza Luis Cabera, one of the best places to read in Mexico City. This is a literary highlight. Aside from being quite a quaint little park with some photography exhibitions and fountains, at the bottom end there's also a bench designed to look like the iconic elephant-swallowed-by-snake imagery of The Little Prince.

Little Prince Volcano, Lake Atitlan, Guatemala

In 1938, Antoine de Saint-Exupéry, author of the beloved children's book, The Little Prince (Le Petit Prince), crashed his plane in Guatemala. During his recuperation, he spent some time on Lake Atitlan, a volcanic lake about three hours outside of Guatemala City. There, as the legend goes, he saw the Cerro de Oro, 'hill of gold,' that inspired a drawing and scene in The Little Prince, published in 1943. The hill, sitting at the edge of the beautiful volcanic lake, does resemble an elephant with a boa trailing off at its head and tail as if it were being consumed. Two hours outside Guatemala City.

Japan

The Little Prince Museum, Hakone, Japan
Address:909 Sengokuhara, Hakone-machi, Ashigarashimo-gun 250-0631 Kanagawa

The Little Prince Museum is the world's only museum devoted to The Little Prince. It was created as part of the worldwide celebration of the birth centennial of author Antoine de Saint-Exupéry. The museum, which explores Saint-Exupéry's life, also features a French townscape and European garden, set within the lush natural beauty of Hakone. The Museum of The Little Prince features outdoor squares and sculptures such as the B-612 Asteroid, the Lamplighter Square, and a sculpture of the Little Prince. The museum grounds additionally feature a Little Prince Park along with the Consuelo Rose Garden; however the main portion of the museum are its indoor exhibits.

Open 9:00AM to 6:00PM (entrance permitted until 5:00PM)
Exhibition hall and Video hall business hours 9:00AM to 5:30PM
The museum may close or change opening hours due to weather conditions.
Closed day: The second Wednesday except March and August
Admission Fee Adults 1600 yen child 700 yen
Hakone is aprox. 90km south-west of Tokyo
Express bus
Approximately 120 minutes by Odakyu Hakone Express Bus from Shinjuku Expressway Bus Terminal. Get off at the Kawamukai bus stop.
For details regarding timetables, fares, etc., please see the Odakyu Hakone Highway Bus home page.

Train and bus
Approximately 30 minutes by Hakone Tozan Bus from the Hakone Yumoto station on the Odakyu line.Get off at the Kawamukai Museum of The Little Prince bus stop.For details regarding timetables, fares, etc., please see the Odakyu Electric Railway and Hakone Tozan Bus home pages.
Car
Approximately 20 minutes from the Tomei Expressway Gotenba Interchange
Parking Capacity:112 vehicles Fee:300yen per day

Middle East

Little Prince Cafe and Bookshop Tel Aviv, Israel

19 King George Street, Tel Aviv

The Little Prince is the perfect literature haven for bookworms. Great for olim, it offers a wide selection of books in Hebrew, Russian, French, and Spanish, as well as an entire room of English literature. With many eclectic, peculiar books, The Little Prince is great for those looking to stray from the typical bookstore selection. The prices are affordable, which has earned this shop a loyal customer base. Get comfortable with a cup of coffee or a glass of cold beer while you browse, or curl up in its dreamy atmosphere to read your latest selection.

Little Prince Graffiti, Tel Aviv, Israel

Fayn Street, Tel Aviv

Graffiti by artists Shlomo Abraham Max Dotan Tihur. Artwork of the prince flying with a flock of birds with the words in Hebrew 'What is essential is invisible to the eye'

Little Prince Illuminated Sculpture, Eilat, Israel

Roni Pelo's sculpture at Little Prince Square in the city of Eilat, Israel.

Little Prince Hostel, Eilat, Israel

Derekh Yotam 1, Eilat, Israel

Located 1.3 km from Kings City in Eilat, Little Prince Hostel features a cash machine and a car park.
This venue is 2 km away from the centre of Eilat. The accommodation is just 1.9 km from Ḥof Mifraz HaShemesh. A bar restaurant is a 5-minute walk away. The hostel is steps away from Spiral Park.

The Little Prince garden in Holon, Israel
Location: Jubilee Grove, Moshe Dayan Street, Holon, Israel

The Story Garden is a unique project of environmental sculpture, in which works inspired by beloved Hebrew children's stories were commissioned from top Israeli artists and then placed in green spaces throughout the city. This ongoing venture - the latest Story Garden was opened in 2014 - is a huge hit with both local families and visitors. Combining poetry and literature with plastic art, these colorful and creative environmental sculptures aim at raising awareness of children's literature, and familiarizing younger generations and new immigrants with the protagonists of Israeli children's literature. Over 40 story gardens are spread across the city, and the sculptures are surrounded by greenery, benches and playgrounds for children. The garden has statues of characters from the book: Little Prince, King, Crown, Lantern Light, Plumber and Railway.
Distance from Tel Aviv 7 miles

Lttle Prince Statue, Tehran Book Garden, Tehran, Iran
Haghani Hwy, Tehran 11369, Iran

The statue is siuated outside the bookstore. Tehran Book Garden consists of various sections including a childrens house, Science section, lounges and book shops.

Little Prince Statue, Fatemi Square, Tehran

The statue of The Little Prince, built by Iranian sculptor Fakhr-e-din Kakavand, has been installed in Tehran's Fatemi Square. Kakavand said the sculpture has been built in a bid to raise people's awareness on environmental protection. 'The little prince holds a withered flower in his hands. He has come to the earth to restore it to life,' he added. The white sculpture is made of fiberglass and is 4.20 meters high.

Russia & Eastern Europe

Little Prince Monument, Abakan, Republic of Khakassia, Russia

Druzhby Narodov St. and Kati Perekreshchenko St. Crossing, Abakan Russia

Sculpture 'The Little Prince' appeared in Abakan in July 2013. Its author – sculptor from Krasnoyarsk Andrey Murzin. Sculpture depicts little prince, who is sitting on his planet and looks into the distance, his scarf sways in the wind, and in the hands – a rose. It is interesting that the planet is a hollow bronze ball outside resembling our moon – with irregularities, craters and volcanoes. The Little Prince himself completely cast in bronze. The whole composition weighs about a ton and set on a square granite pedestal. Since the sculpture is small and very nice, it is not surprising that it has caused such excitement among the kids. And, of course, appeared a tradition – to rub shoe of Little Prince, then make a wish, which will be fulfilled. In addition, the inscription on the ball reminds all passersby that it is necessary to be responsible for the world, our planet, loved ones, and those we have tamed.

The planet is a hollow bronze ball outside resembling our moon – with irregularities, craters and volcanoes. The inscription on the monument reads 'You become responsible, forever, for what you have tamed'
Distance from Moscow 2572 miles

International Saint-Exupéry Centre Ulyanovsk, Russia

Ulyanovsk State University located in Ulyanovsk Russia. City is situated on the Volga River about 440 miles east of Moscow.

Faculty of Culture and Arts
On the 27 February 2012, the university inaugurated its new International Saint-Exupéry Centre, led by its Director, Elena Mironova, an associate professor of French. The center will serve as a permanent museum dedicated to the French author-aviator as well as a cultural and linguistics center for the university. The museum was established with the assistance of Civil Aviation College teacher Nikolai Yatsenko, an author of 12 publications on Saint-Exupéry who personally donated some 6,000 related items. The university's new center will also help support the study of international languages in a city which is promoting itself as a major aerospace and cultural centre. The opening was attended by Ulyanovsk Governor.

Monument of The Little Prince Kazan, Tatarstan, Russia

Ekiyat Puppet Theater. City of Kazan, Peterburgskaya st., 57, Kazan 420107 Russia

Monument of The Little Prince

Moldova's Little Prince Statue, Chisinau, Moldova

Strada Grigore Alexandresc, Chisinau, Moldova

Chișinău also known as Kishinev is the capital and largest city of the Republic of Moldova.

Tucked away rests a small statue of the Little Prince, the famed character of the French writer, Antoine de Saint-Exupéry. The smallest public statue in all of Moldova, the Little Prince captures the whimsy and imagination of all who pass by it.

The Little Prince statue is so tiny that it can easily be missed. The total overall height of the bronze monument is about four inches (11 centimeters), but the Prince himself is even smaller. The statue stands on a metal fence, by a lake in Valea Morilor Park, replacing one of the spheres that adorn the fenceposts. The idea is that all of the spheres of the fence represent the planets mentioned in the novel with the Little Prince standing atop his home planet of asteroid B-612.

Finding the statue can be a little bit tricky, but it's well worth it. At the main entrance of the Valea Morilor Park on Strada Grigore Alexandrescu, look for stairs leading to the embankment with a small metal fence. Once at the fence, the Little Prince lives on the 23rd decorative sphere. Take a picture and touch the bronze planet, as many believe the Little Prince can bring good luck.

Little Prince and The Fox Statue, Lviv, Ukraine

Peizazhna Alley, Kyev, Ukraine, 02000

The Little Prince statue in Picturesque Alley, Kiev, Ukraine Podilskyi District. Art composition of The Little Prince by the sculptor Vladimir Kuznetsov. In November 2010 Kiev French Cultural Centre gave children the mosaic sculpture - figure of the Little Prince.

Little Prince Sculpture, Lazar Globa Park, Dnipro, Ukraine

Karla Marksa Ave. 95, Dnipro 49038, Ukraine

You can find, on the lake, The Little Prince standing on his planet.
Distance from Kiev 281 miles

Asia

Le Petit Prince, Gapyeong-gun, South Korea

Home of Le Petit Prince in Gapyeong-gun, (Gyeonggi-do, Korea) is another amazing place to visit as its just 1 hour drive from Seoul. Petite France, a French cultural village set in the Korean countryside! Petite France serves as both a French cultural village and a youth training facility (Goseong Youth Training Center), and consists of 16 French-style buildings where visitors can lodge and experience French food, clothing, and household culture. The place is amazingly beautiful and the architecture will take you to a land of fairytale.

The concept of Petite France encapsulates 'flowers, stars, and the Little Prince.' The village contains a memorial hall dedicated to the author of the celebrated French novel, Le Petit Prince (1943) and as such it is called the Little Prince theme park. It also has a gallery displaying sculptures and paintings of le coq gaulois (the Gallic rooster), the national symbol of France; Orgel House where a 200-year-old music box plays a sweet melody; a shop that sells herbal and aromatic products; a souvenir shop; and many other locales where you can experience French culture. The village can accommodate up to 200 visitors with 34 guest rooms that hold four to ten people each. Enjoy the marionette experience and hear percussion instruments from around the world, and also enjoy soap bubble experience.

Directions
From Dong Seoul Bus Terminal or Sangbong Bus Terminal. Take an intercity bus to Cheongpyeong. From Cheongpyeong Bus Terminal, take a local bus bound for Petite France. (The Bus has specific times to start) Taxi will cost you 16000won to 18000won($16~$18).
By subway: Go to Cheongpyeong Station either itx/normal subway. From there take Bus to Petite France.
Cheongpyeong is a popular place just outside Seoul because its connecting a lot of destination like Petite France, Garden of Morning Calm, Namisom etc. also hundreds of water resorts and parks. Hotels and Korean restaurants are available near bus terminal.
Admission Fees
Cultural Experience Pass - Adults 10,000 won / Teenagers 8,000 won / Children 6,000 won

Gamcheon Culture Village, Busan, South Korea

203, Gamnae 2-ro, Saha-gu, Busan 49368 South Korea
Busan Gamcheon Village does not require an entrance fee

Gamcheon Culture Village has been labeled the 'Santorini of Korea' due to the colourful houses built around the foothills of Saha-gu mountain. The village portrays a colorful, vibrant view from higher points of Busan which rivals those neighborhoods around the world. The mountainside was not considered a hospitable location to build, and was left as the last remaining affordable location to thousands of refugees from the Korean War. The population swelled in the 1950's as Koreans fled to Busan to escape fighting around the country. They quickly and eagerly built mis-matched shanty homes into the side of the mountain from whatever material they could find. In 2009 the

Dreaming of Machu Picchu in Busan Project commenced. Between it and the subsequent Miro Miro project the Gamcheon neighborhood was given a significant facelift. Over the course of 2 years artist were brought in to paint homes, roofs, and wall murals. 22 statues and pieces of artwork were installed.

Gamcheon's Little Prince is a wall mural of the Little Prince on a building beside a Little Prince statue of him and his fox. The Little Prince statue is placed facing an overlook of Busan Gamcheon Culture Village; gazing at the wonderful colors and ocean below him. Both the Little Prince wall mural and statues are available for free pictures. They are unusual and beautiful, but as the Little Prince is the most popular thing to see in Gamcheon Culture Village there will be a line to get to him. Prepare to wait in line for your chance to sit between The Little Prince and his fox for your chance to have a picture of your back taken.

How to go to Gamcheon Culture Village:
After figuring out how to get to Busan from Seoul (approx 325km, 3 hours by train) follow these directions on how to go to Gamcheon Culture Village.
By Car:
Set Kakao Maps Address to 203, Gamnae 2-ro, Saha-gu, Busan.
By Subway:
Take Orange Line 1 to Toseong Station. Come out via Exit 6. Turn right on the street until you see a hospital on you right. Wait for bus 2 or 2-2, which will take you straight to the village.

La Petit Prince Dessert, Tai Kok Tsui, Hong Kong China

Shop 3,G/F., Kamga Mansion, No.2-16 Pine Street, Tai Kok Tsui, Hong Kong China

This is one of the more popular dessert shop in the district, the dessert is not bad really. It is also a restaurant with the Little Prince theme. It has various types of Little Prince desserts such as lava green tea cakes in star shape.

Little Prince Resort & Spa Siem Reap, Cambodia

Phum wat Svay , Khum Salakomrouk, Siem Reap Cambodia

Welcome to Little Prince Resort & Spa, your Siem Reap 'home away from home.' Little Prince Resort & Spa aims to make your visit as relaxing and enjoyable as possible, which is why so many guests continue to come back year after year. Given the close proximity of popular landmarks, such as Wat Preah Prom Rath (0.7 mi) and The Happy Ranch Horse Farm (1.1 mi), guests of Little Prince Resort & Spa can easily experience some of Siem Reap's most well known attractions.

The Little Prince Restaurant, Udaipur, India

Chand Pol Rd, near Hanuman Ghat, Ambamata, Udaipur, Rajasthan 313001, India

This lovely open-air eatery looking towards the quaint Daiji Footbridge dishes up delicious veg and nonveg meals. There are plenty of Indian options, along with pizzas, pastas and some original variations on the usual multicuisine theme, including Korean and Israeli dishes. The ambience is super relaxed and the service friendly.

The Little Prince Heritage Home, Udaipur,

India

Outside Chand Pole, Near Hanuman Ghat, Naga Nagri Near Pichola Lake, Udaipur 313001 India

Experience the serenity and beauty of the white city while staying at The Little Prince Heritage Home. Just steps away from Chand Pole, our hotel is an oasis in a busy city.Udaipur, in the heart of Rajasthan, is a city of majestic palaces and beautiful lakes. Here, adorning the banks of Lake Pichola and standing witness to the historic City Palace, The Little Prince Heritage Home captures all the romance and splendour of a royal era.

The Little Prince Hotel, Beyoglu, Istanbul, Turkey

Huseyinaga Mahallesi Topcekenler Sokak No. 7 Beylu, Beyoglu, Istanbul, Turkey, 34435

Whether you're a tourist or traveling on business, The Little Prince hotel is a great choice for accommodation when visiting Istanbul. From here, guests can make the most of all that the lively city has to offer. With its convenient location, the property offers easy access to the city's must-see destinations.

Singapore Philatelic Museum, Singapore

23B Coleman Street Singapore Philatelic Museum, Singapore 179807 Singapore

The museum collections start from the 1830s and include stamps from different countries around the world. The museum houses different exhibits and permanent displays. One of the current exhibits is based on the book The Little Prince written by Antoine de Saint-Exupéry, the exhibition celebrates the 75th anniversary of the publication in 2018.

Little Prince Creamery, Singapore Closed

The Little Prince Creamery at Toa Payoh Lor 6 has ceased operations.
Note on their Facebook: It has been an memorable flight for the little prince but regrettably all good things come to an end, and the little prince is leaving his little planet B612 to embark on new journeys ahead from here. The rose has grown strong and sturdy (but not aware;) not needing the glass jar anymore to fend off annoying caterpillars and tiger's claws. The baobabs are not a problem. They are beautiful trees all along. The little prince will miss the many sunrises and sunsets in a day. And who knows, return silently one day.
Till then, take care and see you.

Little Prince-themed cafe, Dipolog City, Zamboanga del Norte, Philippines

Boulevard Gateway, Rizal Ave, Dipolog City, Zamboanga del Norte, Philippines

Chapters Book Cafe in Dipolog The Little Prince (Le Petit Prince) is the most famous work of the French writer and poet Antoine de Saint-Exupéry. Chapters book cafe dipolog the little prince mural So stumbling into a Little Prince-themed cafe was an unexpected surprise during a trip to Dipolog, Zamboanga del Norte. Chapters Book Cafe, located along Sunset Boulevard, has the same childlike dreamy quality of the book. Bright cheerful interiors and lots of whimsical details decorate the space. Hardbound books hang next to lamps from the ceiling, while artwork and famous lines from the book are scrawled on the walls and tables.

Australia

Little Prince Eating House & Bar, Traralgon, Victoria, Australia

58 Hotham St, Traralgon, Victoria 3844 Australia

Little Prince is a class restaurant with good vegetarian options.
Distance from Melbourne 102 miles

The Little Prince, Restaurant, Wollongong, NSW, Australia

Globe Lane, Wollongong, New South Wales 2500, Australia

Bar, Fusion, Australian, features outdoor Seating, Seating, Serves Alcohol.
Distance from Sydney 51 miles, Lake Haven 112 miles

The Little Prince Espresso, Brisbane, Australia

8 Annerley Road, Brisbane, Queensland Australia

CUISINES : Cafe, Australian MEALS: Breakfast FEATURES: Seating, Takeout.

Africa

The Antoine de Saint-Exupéry Museum, Tarfaya, Morocco

The Antoine de Saint Exupéry Museum is a museum of air mail in Tarfaya, Morocco. Founded in 2004, it is devoted to author and aviator Antoine de Saint Exupery who lived there for two years, from 1927 to 1929, and found there the inspiration for much of his literary work. In 1927, Saint-Exupéry was appointed chief of the stopover airfield in the Tarfaya region, formerly known as Cape Juby. Tarfaya opened the museum in 2004 to recount the history of the aviation company Aeropostale and its route from Toulouse to Saint Louis, Senegal. The museum is the principal attraction for visitors to the town. A monument representing a Bréguet 14 dedicated to the memory of Antoine de Saint-Exupéry takes place in front of the museum.
Distance from Rabat 670 miles

The Baobab Restaurant, Arusha, Tanzania
44/1 Serengeti Road, Arusha Tanzania

The Baobab Restaurant is uniquely designed and offers a comfortable and enjoyable dining experience. Our Chefs creatively prepare exotic and delicious meals with fresh and natural ingredients giving guests a flavor of both Tanzanian and International cuisine. Saint-Exupéry wrote The Little Prince and in it the Baobab trees are evil... these are lovely Baobabs. Clean, well attended and excellent food. Yes, even the Little Prince would agree.

Wadi El Natrun, Egypt

Wadi El Natrun is a depression in northern Egypt that is located 75ft below sea level and 125ft below the Nile River level. The valley contains several alkaline lakes, natron-rich salt deposits, salt marshes and freshwater marshes.

The environs of Wadi Natrun have been identified as the likely site of where the plane of French aviator Antoine de Saint-Exupéry crashed on December 30, 1935. After miraculously surviving the crash, he and his plane's mechanic nearly died of thirst before being rescued by a nomad. Saint-Exupéry documented his experience in his book ' Wind, Sand and Stars'. The event is thought to have inspired his masterpiece, The Little Prince.
Distance from Cairo 78 miles, El Sadat City 27 miles

The Little Prince Luxury Camp, Merzouga, Morocco
Ksar Merzouga 52202, Kamkamia Merzouga, 52202 Merzouga, Morocco

The Little Prince Luxury Camp, is an ideal base for your Amazigh Berber Desert adventure, with spectacular craggy mountains in the distance, endless dunes, and crystalline wadis. It is only a one hour drive away from Erfoud. The camp is sprawled across 10-acres of silken sands, secluded 6 km within the vast isolation of the Merzouga desert. 4 luxurious Berber style tents await those who seek the ultimate desert adventure vacation at the finest Merzouga Luxury Tents The Little Prince Luxury Camp.
Distance from Casablanca 204 miles

Le Petit Prince Hotel and Restaurant, Merzouga, Morocco
B.p 48, Merzouga 52202 Morocco

A family run establishment in the heart of Merzouga at the foot of the Erg Chebbi dunes. Hotel rooms, camping cars, campground, camel treks, desert bivouac, excursions, and tours of Morocco.

Petit Poucet Restaurant, Casablanca, Morocco
86 Boulevard Mohamed V, Casablanca 20000 Morocco

It is now served by the relatively new Casa tramway line, but its famous former customers include the writers St. Exupéry and Albert Camus. Walk in their footsteps.

Antoine de Saint-Exupéry School, Saint-Louis du Sénégal
Quai Roume Nord
BP 332, Saint-Louis du Sénégal

The Antoine-de-Saint-Exupéry French school is a French educational institution abroad.
It is an international school, which currently has 141 students, representing several nationalities
The Saint-Exupéry establishment welcomes children from 3 years up to high school.

Saint-Exupéry School of Dakar, Senegal
Route de N'gor – Almadies, (opposite the International University)

Senegalese private primary school with French curriculum

Lycée Saint-Exupéry de Ouagadougou, Burkina Faso, Africa
Koulouba, Ouagadougou, Burkina Faso

The Lycée français Saint-Exupéry is a French international school in Ouagadougou, Burkina Faso. It serves levels maternelle through lycée. It was established in 1975. The secondary school is in the centre of the city while the primary school is in proximity to the hôtel Indépendance.

Space

Le Petit Prince, Space

Mar 12, 2002

'Le Petit Prince,' the well-loved fable of a little prince who is a galactic voyager, will go into space in May in an unusual tribute to its French author. French astronaut Philippe Perrin told reporters Tuesday that the book would be part of his luggage when he travels to the International Space Station. The copy was given to him by Francois Agay, Saint-Exupéry's nephew.

2578 Saint-Exupéry Asteroid

2578 Asteroid Saint-Exupéry, discovered in November 1975 by Russian astronomer Tamara Smirnova and provisionally cataloged as Asteroid 1975 VW3, was renamed in the author-aviator's honour. The asteroid's was first identified as 1952 HG2 at McDonald Observatory in Texas. One month later, it was also observed at the Palomar Observatory in May 1952.

Saint-Exupéry is an asteroid, approximately 17 kilometres in diameter, a large rock that orbits the Sun mainly between the orbits of Mars and Jupiter. It is a member the Eros family, the largest asteroid family of the outer main belt consisting of nearly 10,000 known members. The asteroid orbits the Sun once every 5 years and 2 months (1,900 days). They tend to be an irregular shaped but Ceres asteroid is known to be spherical in shape but because it doesn't clear its path round the Sun, it is only a dwarf planet. The absolute magnitude of the object is 11.5 which is the brightness of the object. A higher absolute magnitude means that the object is faint whereas a very low number means it is very bright. The Longitude of Ascending Node of the object is 55.70215 degrees. The Argument of Perihelion is 335.7346. It is the angle along the orbit of a planet or other Solar System object as measured from the ascending node (analogous to right ascension and longitude) The mean anomoly is 207.42392, is the angular distance of the planet from the perihelion or aphelion.

46610 Bésixdouze Asteroid

Provisional designation 1993 TQ1, is a bright background asteroid from the inner regions of the asteroid belt approximately 2 kilometers in diameter. It was discovered on 15 October 1993, by Japanese amateur astronomers Kin Endate and Kazuro Watanabe at the Kitami Observatory in eastern Hokkaidō, Japan. The asteroid was named after 'B-612', home of The Little Prince.

Bésixdouze is a non family asteroid from the main belt's background population. It orbits the Sun in the inner main-belt at a distance of 1.9–2.7 AU once every 3 years and 5 months, 1,249 days. The asteroid was first identified as 1986 RU at Crimea Nauchinij in a single image taken in September 1986.

The name was suggested by F. Hemery and Jiri Grygar as a reference to the French novella The Little Prince. The title character lived on an asteroid named B-612, which is the number 46610 written in hexadecimal notation. Bésixdouze B-six-twelve is one way to pronounce B-612 in French. Like the asteroid in The Little Prince Besixdouze was first observed in a single night, several years before its official discovery. The official naming citation was published by the Minor Planet Centre on 20 November 2002.

1 Petit-Prince Moon

Eugenia I Petit-Prince is the larger, outer moon of asteroid 45 Eugenia. It was discovered in 1998 by astronomers at the Canada-France-Hawaii Telescope on Mauna Kea, Hawaii. Initially, it received the provisional designation S/1998 (45) 1. Petit-Prince was the first asteroid moon to be discovered with a ground-based telescope.

Petit-Prince is 13 km in diameter, compared to 45 Eugenia's 214km. It takes five days to complete an orbit around Eugenia. The discoverers chose the name in honour of Empress Eugenie's son, the Prince Imperial. However, they also intended an allusion to the children's book The Little Prince which is about a prince who lives on an asteroid. In their submission of the name to the IAU the discovers justified the double meaning by arguing for similarities between the Prince Imperial and the Little Prince:

Both princes were young and adventurous, and had little fear of danger. Both were of rather small stature. They both left the confines of their cozy little worlds (asteroid B612 for the Little Prince and Chislehurst for the Prince Imperial). They both then undertook long journeys to end up in Africa, whereupon they both meet rather violent deaths ... And in both cases they lay alone for one night each after 'death' and then returned back home.

Other Little Prince sights

Staircase in Seoul, South Korea
Ice cream shop, Las Vegas
Alley, Hamadan Province, Iran
Indian restaurant, Udaipur, India
House front, Valaraiso, Chile

Garage door mural, El Escorial, Spain
Building, Conthey, Switzerland
School, Chivay, Peru
Merry-go-round, Alsace, France
Wall painting, Havana, Cuba
House front, Brussels, Belgium
Inn, Abengourou, Cote d'Ivoire
Exupery house, Buenos Aires, Argentina
Fountain, hills above Rio de Janeiro, Brazil
Street, Montesson, a suburb of Paris

The Little Prince Translated Languages and Dialects

Aalsters, Abkhaz, Afrikaans, Albanian, Ancient Egyptian, Altay, Old English, Old French, Ancient Greek, Alur, Amharic, Arabic Algerian, Arabic Emirates, Arabic Morrocan, Arabic Lebanese, Arabic Palestine, Arabic Tunisian, Aragonese, Aramaic, Aranese, Armenian, Armenian Western, Aromunian, Azerbaijani, Azerbaijani Southern, Assamesse, Asturian, Aymara, Badish-Alemannic, Balinese, Bambara, Barese Italian, Bashkir, Basel German, Basque, Bavarian, Béarnese, Belarusian, Bengali, Bergamasque, Berlinian, Bernesse German, Bikol, Burmese, Bolognese, Bolze, Borain, Bosnian, Breton, Bulgarian, Bulgarian Banat, Burgundian, Buryat, Chavacano, Chinese, Ciluba, Danish, Dari, German, German Braille, Digorian, Drents, Dusseldorf German, Alsation, English, English Aurebesh, Eoniavian, Ore Mountain German, Esperanto, Estonian, Extramaduran, Eupen German, Faroese, Filipino, Finnish, Florentine, Franconian, Franko-Provençal, French, French Morse, Frisian, Friulian, Galician, Gallo, Galluresse, Gascon, Genoese, Georgian, Greek, Greenlandic, Guarani, Gujarati, Hakka, Hawaiian, Hebrew, Hessian, Hindi, Hunsrik German, Ido, Indonesian, Irish Gaelic, Icelandic, Italilian, Yakut, Japanese, Yiddish, Yiddish Warsaw, Kabardian, Calabrian, Kambaata, Kannada, Cantonese, Karaim, Karelian, Karen, Carinthian, Kazakh, Qashqay, Kashubian, Catalan, Catalan Braille, Khmer, Kinyarwanda, Kyrgz, Kirundi, Klingon, Koalib, Cologne Germany, Komkani, Korean, Koryak, Cornish, corsican, Creole French Guyana, Creole Guadeloupe, Creole Haiti, Creole Jamaica, Creole Cape Verde, Creole Martinique, Creole Mauritius, Creole Reunion, Creole Rodrigues, Creole Sao Tome, Creole Seychelles, Croation, Croation Burgenland, Croation Kajkavian, Kumyk, Kurdish

Hewrami, Kurdish Kelhuri, Kurdish Sorani, Ladin Ampezzo, Ladin Badia Velley, Ladin Gherdeina, Languedoc, Lanna, Laotian, Laz Ardesen, Laz Hopa, Latin, Lemko, Leonese, Latgalian, Liegeois, Limburgian Northern, Limburgian Southern, Limousin, Lithuanian, Livornese Italian, Lothringian, Luxemburgian, Macedonian, Malagasy, Malay, Malayan, Majorcan, Maltese, Mantua Italian, Manx, Mapudungun, Marathi, Mari, Marquesan, Mashi, Masurian, Maya Kaqchikel, Maya Yucatecan, Milanese, Mirandese, Middle English, Middle High German, Modenese Italian, Molisano Italian, Molise Slavic, Mongolian Cyrillic, Mongolian Traditional, Nahuatl, Neapolitan, Nepali, Lower Alemannic, Dutch, Normand, Norwegian, Norwegian, Nynorsk, Upper Austrian, Occitan, Oriya, Ossetian, Otomi, Papiamento, Parmesan, Pashto, Pennsylvania German, Persian Farsi, Persian Tajikistan, Perugino Italian, Pesarese Italian (Pesaro), Palatine-Saarlandian, Piacentino, Picardian, Piedmontese, Low German Hummling, Low German North, Plautdietsch, Poitevin-Saintongeais, Polish, Polish Wielkopolska, Portuguese, Portuguese Braille, Portuguese Brazil, Prussian, Provincal, Punjabi, Quechua, Rajasthani, Romansh Grischun, Romanish Surmiran, Romanish Sursilvan, Romanish Vallader, Reggiano, Romagnol, Romanes Gypsy, Romanesco, Ruhr German,
Romanian, Romanian Moldovian, Russian, Saalandian, Salentino, Saami Inari, Saami Northern, Saami Skolt, Sango, Sanskrit, Sardinian-Corsican, Sardinian Campidanese, Sardinian Logudorese, Sardinian Southern, Sassaresse, Sassaresse Castellanese, Saterland Frisian, Silesian, Scottish Gaelic, Svabian, Swedish, Scots, Serbian, Seto, Setswana, Sinhalese, Singlish, Sicilian, Slovak, Slovene, Slovene Prekmurje, Somali, Soninke, Sorbian Lower, Sorbian Upper, Spanglish, Spanish Aljamiado, Spanish Braille, Spanish, Andalusian, Spanish Murcian, Sranantongo, Strasbourgian,

South Jutlandic, South Tyrolean, Sundanese, Swahili, Tabarchin Sardinia, Tajik, Tahitian, Tamasheq, Tamazight Kabylia, Tamazight Morocco, Tamil, Tarahumara, Tatar, Telugu, Tandasque Tende, Teramano Italian, Ticinese, Tetum, Thai, Tibetan, Tigrinya, Tyrolean, Toba, Tongan, Totanac, Trentine, Triestinian, Czech, Chechen, Chukchi, Chuvash, Turkish, Turkish Braille, Turkish Colour Alphabet, Turkish Gokturkish, Turkish Denizli, Turkish Ottoman, Turkish Cyprus, Turkmen, Tzeltal, Tzotzil, Udehe, Uyghur, Uilta, Ukranian, Hungarian, Hungarian Runes, Urdu, Uropi, Uzbek, Val Di Cornia Italian, Valencian, Venetian, Venetian Montebelluna, Venetian Verona, Venetian Vicenza, Venetian Venice, Vietnamese, Vogherese Italian, Welsh, Walliser German, Walloon, Walloon Namur, Wayuu, Welche, Western Palatine-Saarlandian, Viennese, Wolof, Xhosa, Zazaki, Cimbrian German, Zulu, Zurich German.

Celebrity Endorsements of The Little Prince

If I would use anything from 'The Little Prince,' even some little quote, it's all copyrighted in France. Like Walt Disney in this country, it's a national treasure. Peter Sis

I got the boot once from Stanley Donen. The film was called The Little Prince. Julie Harris

I had a moment - and I don't know if it was funny, necessarily, but I realized the effect I could have on people - when I was doing a production of 'The Little Prince,' and I played the snake. Lennon Parham

I am afraid that people will think I re-illustrated 'The Little Prince,' when really, it was more a tribute to him as a dedicated pilot and a man who believed in the goodness of people. Peter Sis

When I was about 12 or 13, my father gave me 'The Little Prince.' He was making sure that I knew it was a special book. I'd seen the name of Antoine de Saint-Exupery, but to me it seemed a very French name, and I was not excited about him as a person. Peter Sis

I went to the sort of summer camp that had gender-blind casting, and so when I was about nine years old, I played the Little Prince on stage. I was one of seven actors — I use the term loosely — to share the part. I think I had about two scenes, and the pilot I was playing opposite was much older than I was, and I had a huge crush on him. Needless to say, I forgot all my lines, and the next year, when the play was The

Wizard of Oz, I was relegated to the part of an evil stepsister, a part that doesn't actually exist.
Emma Straub, author:

I can't remember the very first time I laid eyes on Le Petit Prince. Growing up in Paris, I'm sure it was around me in many forms from the time I moved there at the age of four. I do remember, however, really reading it for the first time, and how it made me feel. I was in the fifth grade, still in Paris, and I remember feeling so utterly understood by this character, feeling so very connected to him. Childhood can be such a lonely time, and le Petit Prince captures it so beautifully. For many I believe it is the first experience with nostalgia and melancholy, a gateway to these feelings you continue to experience as an adolescent and as an adult. Kelsey Smith, Assistant Editor, Scribner:

Like a number of other famous children's books, I grew up reading The Little Prince in Russian instead of English. It was one of many tattered Soviet-era books my parents brought with them when they emigrated from the USSR and insisted I read these editions, instead of the smoother, glossier American versions. They tell me that The Little Prince, like so many other Western texts that slowly made their way into Russia after Stalin's death in the '50s, was overwhelmingly refreshing with its emphasis on the individual quest and nonconformity. It represented total escapism. It's a book that's stayed with me more strongly in my visual rather than narrative memory, so I recently decided to reread it (you can imagine the sympathetic looks I got on the subway). More than anything, what stunned me now was the book's dedication — "All grown-ups were children first. (But few of them remember it). So I correct my dedication: To Leon Werth — When he was a little boy."

Elianna Kan, Senior Editor, The American Reader:

I've never actually read The Little Prince, and I've only heard it read from once, in the summer of 2011, when an excerpt from it served as the reading at a wedding I officiated between two writer friends of mine, on the gorgeous and steep lawn of a certain bourbon distillery in Kentucky. The reading they chose from The Little Prince included these lovely lines of dialogue, the fox speaking to the prince: Matt Bell, author

I would say: Simplicity is truth--and truth is simple. Our problem is that we no longer see the forest for the trees; that for all our knowledge, we have lost the path to wisdom. This is also the idea behind Saint-Exupery's The Little Prince which shows how the cleverness of our age causes us, ironically, to overlook the essential, while the Little Prince, who hasn't the faintest idea about all this cleverness, ultimately sees more and better. Pope Benedict XV1

Antoni Porowski, star of Netflix's Queer Eye

At a Barnes & Noble event, September 2019 on Twitter, 'Excited to meet everyone and pick up all the copies of A Little Prince in stock'

Intervied in Hunger Magazine, June 2018
You can have five people, dead or alive, at a dinner party – who do you choose?

'Oh my gosh! Only five? I'd have Johnny Cash, Jack Kerouac, Yoko Ono, Patti Smith and Antoine de Saint-Exupéry, who wrote The Little Prince.'

Raya Abirached & Hend Sabri Read 'The Little Prince' For Save The Children Charity

The reading took place live on IWC Schaffhausen's Instagram Account on Tuesday, April 21. Hend Sabri and Raya Abirached have came together with other stars to read extracts from 'The Little Prince' for IWC's beneficial virtual storytelling series. By reading chapters from The Little Prince Hend Sabri and Raya Abirached were hoping to inspire, entertain and support, as well as lift spirits during this period of uncertainty. Indian actress Sonam Kapoor, Italian actor Pierfrancesco Favino and Chinese actor Zhang Ruo were the other ambassadors taking turns to read extracts from Antoine de Saint-Exupéry's most famous literary work.

Meghan Markle shared how she loves The Little Prince

'I have long been obsessed with this book, and specifically with The Little Fox. Even if I don't revisit the entire existential text (masked as a children's book), the chapter of The Little Fox unearths a truth in me that is always worth the check-in. And if my vouching for it doesn't give it the badass quality you're looking for, the film remake is due to be released soon with a star-studded cast. So there ya go, fancy pants.'

Emma Watson is an English actress and model. She rose to prominence portraying Hermione Granger in the Harry Potter film series.

What is your favorite book and why?
My dad read me The BFG by Roald Dahl when I was younger. I'm really fond of that book. Le Petit Prince by Antoine de Saint-Exupéry. I like books that aren't just lovely but that have memories in themselves. Just like playing a song, picking up a book again that has memories can take you back to another place or another time.

Indiana, mayor and 2020 Democratic presidential candidate Pete Buttigieg

Bookseller One Grand Books asked celebrities to name the ten titles they'd take to a desert island. Indiana, mayor and 2020 Democratic presidential candidate Pete Buttigieg included The Little Prince.

'It's touching, it's about innocence and exploration, and it's sad but also uplifting'

James Dean, Actor,

It's a little known fact James Dean, the all American 'rebel' and international symbol of a Hollywood life cut short, was a talented writer. He had a passion for poetry and his favourite book was The Little Prince. The book is immortalised on his tombstone with his favourite quote: 'What is essential is invisible to the eye.' Dean's writing wasn't visible to the eyes of the public, so here's a look at that story - not of the actor but of the writer. Dean deeply identified with the book and took it with him any time he moved. The book was so important to Dean that his good friend, biographer, and possible lover, William Bast wrote about it in an inscription on Dean's memorial near his crash site. The inscription starts off with Dean's favorite line from the book, ' What is essential is invisible to the eye'. It is then followed by Bast's explanation, 'This quotation from Antoine de Saint Exupery's 'The Little Prince' was probably James Dean's favourite. It seemed to hold a deep and private significance for him, and he read it often especially with those he loved.'

Little Prince Spin-offs

The Little Prince Returns
Yoram Selbst

Paperback – 9 Dec. 2018

This book tells the tale of what happened after that moment, of the blossoming of friendship and understanding between two unlikely companions as, over many cups of tea brewed with the last of their water, they shared their life experiences and their inner feelings. It is an attempt to recapture the unforgettable magic of that earlier encounter.
The author begins his story with a heartfelt letter to Saint-Exupéry thanking him for writing the original story of The Little Prince and regretting the many, long years for which his presence on Earth has been absent.

Now the time has come for the reunion. Selbst has just stolen a ship from his captain and he is alone at sea when he spies The Little Prince in a small boat. The sailor named Dror rescues him. They carry on many philosophical discussions in which the Prince alternately enchants and befuddles Dror with his questions and explanations. When the ship loses power and appears lost at sea, the two unlikely companions become truly bonded. Will Dror find the hidden meaning of life? Does his life end on a stolen ship at sea or will he be rescued and sent back to his ordinary life on Earth?

The elderly prince: A tale for big kids
Ricardo Marti Ruiz

Paperback – 26 July 2017

Time waits for no one, and the little prince is no exception. In fact, he's grown quite a lot since you last met: his humble asteroid is now an lovely satellite, and many of his personal relationships have changed as well. As he himself puts it, 'Life remains just as pretty, but not just the same'. Share some time with an old friend in this charming sequel to the all time classic, and discover what it takes to be a child, and why everyone deserves to have a happy ending.

The Return of the Young Prince
A.G. Roemmers

Hardcover – 9 Jan. 2016

Few stories are as widely read and as universally cherished by children and adults alike as The Little Prince. But even princes from faraway planets eventually grow up. No longer content with his tiny planet, the young prince sets off once again to explore the universe. And so begins another remarkable journey into the secrets and joys of living a meaningful life. A charming fable for all ages, this wonderful follow-up to the beloved classic overflows with love and wisdom, a true celebration of life as it should be lived in all its beauty and joy.

A Guide for Grown-Ups: Essential Wisdom from the Collected Works of Antoine de Saint-Exupéry (Little Prince)

Hardcover – 6 Oct. 2015

What does it mean to be a grown-up? How do we find happiness, joyful friendships, and love that lasts? Culled from the full works of the author of The Little Prince here is subtle, radiant wisdom that has charmed and enlightened the hearts of generations. This is a beautifully presented volume of tidbits and quotes from the collected works of the author, the insights are funny thoughtful and sometimes moving. As there is only really a sentence per page if you try to read this book all at once you miss the significance and insights of some of the quotes, instead this is a great book to have by your bed to read a little of each night.

The Tiny Rose: One More Tale Inspired by The Little Prince
Simone Bondroit

Paperback – 8 Jun. 2018

Following on from The Little Prince by Antoine de Saint-Exupéry, this is another one of the loveliest yet saddest stories of the world. It is about the journey of a little rose through landscapes of the human soul. Like the little prince the tiny rose is alone on her journey. And like him, she also discovers a secret. It is a courageous search for the roots of love, a story of an unusual friendship – and of the reality of growing up. It is an allegory on gently keeping hold of happiness. And last but not least, it is about reading a book again without knowing its outcome.

In her book, Simone Bondroit sensitively and captivatingly brings to life the figure of the rose from Antoine de Saint-Exupéry's masterpiece. It is for all those who have always wanted a sequel to The Little Prince in a convincingly modeled new edition and who want to immerse themselves once again in the magical world of the original with its uniquely touching language.

Travels with the Little Prince board book
Antoine de Saint-Exupéry

1 May 2016

This classic, beloved tale is re-imagined as a beautiful, tabbed board book, with original illustrations and simple text.

Meet the Little Prince board book
Antoine de Saint-Exupéry

1 Nov. 2015

Hello, I am the Little Prince. Bonjour, je suis le Petit Prince. Meet the Little Prince and read about his tiny planet in both English and French! This classic, beloved tale is re-imagined as a beautiful, padded board book, with original illustrations and a playful, sweet design.

Counting with the Little Prince board book
Antoine de Saint-Exupéry

1 Nov. 2015

No story is more beloved by children and grown-ups alike than this wise, enchanting fable. Parents can share this classic tale with their babies and toddlers as it is re-imagined in this beautiful, sturdy board book. The youngest readers will delight in discovering one prince, two sheep, three trees and so on until they reach the final page where they lift the flap for a surprise.

The Little Prince Coloring Book: Beautiful Images for You to Color

Antoine de Saint-Exupéry

Paperback – 1 May 2016
This magical coloring book features original illustrations and memorable quotes from Antoine de Saint-Exupery's masterpiece, The Little Prince. The delicate and highly detailed line illustrations are waiting to be brought to life with your favorite colored pencils or fine markers. Little Prince fans of all ages will find pleasure in this sophisticated and creative book.

The Little Prince Read-Aloud Storybook: Abridged Original Text
Antoine de Saint-Exupéry

Hardcover – 17 Nov. 2015

The Little Prince, adapted for children and illustrated with the magnificent original images from the film. A book full of tenderness, designed to help youngsters discover the magic of the universal masterpiece by Saint-Exupéry.

The Little Prince by Antoine de Saint-Exupéry Novel Study Workbook
Elizabeth M. Porter
Paperback – 22 Jun. 2019

With its profound messages of love and connection, The Little Prince is a story that transcends age and time. All of the activities are designed to promote critical thinking in the target language and analysis as well as cross curricular extensions. Activities include skills in comparing and contrasting, in depth discussion, history extensions, critical thinking activities, and more. This is a great resource for classroom teachers and homeschool read-aloud families alike.

A Study Guide for Antoine de Saint-Exupéry's The Little Prince
Cengage Learning Gale

Paperback 25 July 2017

Cengage Learning Gale

A Study Guide for The Little Prince, excerpted from Gale's acclaimed Novels for Students. This concise study guide includes plot summary; character analysis; author biography; study questions; historical context; suggestions for further reading; and much more. For any literature project, trust Novels for Students for all of your research needs.

Teacher Guide and Novel Unit for The Little Prince: Lessons on Demand
John Pennington

Paperback – 8 July 2017

The lessons on demand series is designed to provide ready to use resources for novel study. In this book you will find key vocabulary, student organizer pages, and assessments. This guide is divided into two sections. Section one is the teacher section which consists of vocabulary and activities. Section two holds all of the student pages, including assessments and graphic organizers.

The Little Prince (Sparknotes)

Antoine de Saint-Exupery

Paperback 1 Nov. 2004 Antoine de Saint-Exupery

Today's most popular study guides-with everything you need to succeed in school. Written by Harvard students for students, since its inception "SparkNotes(TM) has developed a loyal community of dedicated users and become a major education brand. They feature the most current ideas and themes, written by experts. - They're easier to understand, because the same people who use them have also written them. - The clear writing style and edited content enables students to read through the material quickly, saving valuable time.

Discovering the Hidden Wisdom of The Little Prince: In Search of Saint-Exupéry's Lost Child
Pierre Lassus
Hardcover – 24 Aug. 2017

In this elegant, carefully argued book, Pierre Lassus reexamines the story of The Little Prince against the facts of Saint-Exupéry's own extraordinary life, from his cherished but fatherless childhood in aristocratic poverty to his career as a pioneering pilot. His plane had broken down in the desert before. He had adopted a fox, when posted at the Spanish fort of Cape Juby, in southern Morocco. He had known the world of business before becoming pilot; he had also known unrequited love. Like his little protagonist's, his body was never found after his plane disappeared in World War II. He was working on his spiritual autobiography when he died, and there too, Lassus finds resonances and keys to the understated spirituality of his last great book.

The Lawyer and The Little Prince
A. Joseph Tandet

Paperback 4 Dec. 2008

Joseph Tandet, practicing entertainment attorney and a theatre and film producer in New York City, chronicles the adventures and misadventures he experienced bringing the classic story, The Little Prince, to the big screen. He relates how a little yeshiva boy from Brooklyn, growing up with sparse parental encouragement, attended college and law school, litigated a string of negligence cases, and went on to surmount the daunting obstacles and experience the heights of the entertainment world and Hollywood. Tandet convinced the French publisher, Gallimard, and the Saint-Exupéry family to sign a boilerplate contract under the pretense that Gene Kelley had already signed on as the leading man. Armed with nothing but nerve and chutzpah, he was able to make his way through the valley of the moguls and convince Paramount Pictures to produce a feature-length film based upon the popular story.Tandet reveals the conversations he had with directors, actors, writers, and others he met on his path to taking the magical, musical fable based upon Antoine de Saint-Exupéry's story from an idea to a feature film. This engaging memoir provides captivating inside details regarding a film that is still popular, decades after its release.

The Little Prince Series 24 Book Set
Various Authors

Published 2012 Lerner Publishing Group

Discover a modern, graphic-novel take on a timeless classic The Little Prince is adapted from the TV series based on the classic masterpiece by Antoine de Saint-Exupéry.

The universe is in danger: the stars are going out one by one along the path of the Serpent. The Little Prince, determined not to let evil rule the galaxy, leaves his asteroid and his beloved Rose to embark on a monumental quest. Accompanied by his faithful friend Fox, he will discover vast worlds set off kilter by strange rules and dangerous strife and will use his extraordinary gifts to help bring balance to each planet.

Leon Werth and Antoine de Saint-Exupery - The dedication in many languages
Compiled by Shlomo Lerman

Jerusalem, 2015

The Little Princess: On the trail of the Little Prince
Peter Frank Zuuring

Hardcover 1 Aug. 2014

For the last 70 years people everywhere, both young and old, have been delighted by Antoine de Saint-Exupery's 'The Little Prince'. Its simplicity and innocence reveal some fundamental values that we can apply to our own lives to make a better world. After the Prince mysteriously disappears, Saint-Exupery calls on the reader to let him know if he has returned. Well, in a sense he has, if a young girl's journey is to be believed. She might have imagined it all. But then again, maybe not… The original of this book, 'The Little Princess' was first published by To Be Continued…in English in The Netherlands, June 2015. This novella is a work of fiction. Based on Characters, places, names etc. that are found in the public domain as the original copyrights for text and illustrations have now expired as the first published work of 'The Little Prince' in French and English in the USA was in 1943… 70+ years ago. All characters/illustrations not found in Exupéry's novella are copyrighted as of 2014.

The Return of The Little Prince
Ysatis Desaint-Simon

Paperback 9 Feb. 2004

A Sequel to Le petit prince.

Antoine de Saint-Exupéry Biographies

Antoine de Saint-Exupéry: The Life and Death of the Little Prince
Paul Webster

Paperback – 8 July 1994

Since his mysterious disappearance in an unarmed reconnaissance plane in July 1944, Antoine de Saint-Exupéry has been the focus for romantic fascination. This biography brings back to life a 20th-century hero - a man of passion who combined the dangerous career of pioneering aviator with that of bestselling author of classic works such as The Little Prince.

The Pilot and the Little Prince: The Life of Antoine de Saint-Exupéry
Peter Sis

Hardcover – 3 July 2014

The beautifully illustrated life story of Antoine de Saint-Exupéry - an aviator, adventurer, pioneer and war hero, as well as the author of one of the world's most beloved children's books, The Little Prince. 'Sís' works are less picture books than little miracles of design, a craft he now devotes to a biography of Antoine de Saint-Exupéry. That de Saint-Exupéry's life was interesting in its own right growing up fatherless, pioneering ever-more dangerous airmail delivery routes, flying in WWII is nearly besides the point, because Sís has created such a compelling, multilayered visual treat. Sís's handling of the aviator s last flight and disappearance strikes just the right notes of mystery, majesty, and quiet wonder that connect the life and longings of Saint-Exupéry to those of his young, fictional friend. Brilliant bookmaking.

In Search of the Little Prince : The Story of Antoine de Saint-Exupéry
Bimba Landmann

Paperback – 30 Nov. 2014

This lyrical picture book biography tells the story of its author, Antoine de Saint-Exupéry. As a child, Antoine dreamed of flying. His dream was realised when he became a pilot, first serving France during World War I, then working as an international mail courier. As he wrote letters to his family describing the foreign countries he visited, he soon discovered that writing contained its own sense of adventure. His stories showed a childlike fascination with the world, culminating with The Little Prince, one of the best-selling books ever published. Bimba Landmanns biography is paired with whimsical yet profound illustrations, wonderfully capturing Saint-Exupérys personality. This book will give fresh insight into the life of a cherished author.

Antoine de Saint-Exupéry: His Life and Times
Curtis Cate

Paperback – 1 July 1990

The book is very well written, with rich material.

Knight Of The Air: The Life And Works Of Antoine de Saint-Exupéry
Maxwell Austin Smith

Hardcover – 19 Aug. 2011

Saint-Exupéry: A Biography
Stacy Schiff
Paperback – 7 Nov. 1996

A fascinating account of the life of one of the century's great eccentrics - the brilliant Antoine de Saint-Exupéry. Born in 1900 of impoverished aristocracy, he swiftly developed a mania for aviation, despite his chaotic mind and total technological incompetence. He flew reconnaissance missions in the War and wrote some strange and wonderful books, including the classic children's story, between theatrically executed airplane crashes. He died in the air in 1944, and his brief life instantly acquired mythical status. 'Every facet of Saint-Exupery's short and dramatic life is covered in this fascinating biography. This is Stacy Schiff's first book, but she writes with all the skill, assurance and mastery of an old literary hand. If there was such a thing as a prize for a first biography, I would nominate this book.

The Rose that captivated The Little Prince, Consuelo de Saint-Exupéry
Abigail Suncin

The world is acquainted with the beautiful story concerning Le Petite Prince when he ran away from his Rose…It is time for everyone in the world to know the real story of the Rose that captivated Le Petite Prince, which is in addition very interesting, It is an incentive to reach our most cherished of dreams transcendental from the same Petite Prince and be able to see the light on Earth. Consuelo Suncín de Saint-Exupéry was a truly exceptional woman, she pushed forward ahead of her time to overcome all obstacles and arrive to other horizons in harmony with her ideals. Latin americans ought to be proud of this extraordinary woman, who was capable to inspire one of the most acclaimed literature works in the world, it is considered a legacy to humanity for its worthy spiritual message.

The biography that Abigail Suncín writes of Consuelo is very different from all the others ever written, since there is one chapter in the life of Consuelo that other authors have not viewed with interest. It is that aspect on the year she spent in Oppede, a place to which she fled seeking refuge from the Second World War. In that place she gained a spiritual experience that completely changed her outlook on life, and it surely, greatly influenced Saint-Exupéry's inspiration when they met again after a year of being apart. When they return to live together in New York, he began to write 'The Little Prince', to which Abigail referred as the couple's only child. Gladys Abigail Alvarado Suncín, granddaughter nephew of Consuelo Suncín, the author, who since the presentation of this literary work learned that her passion in life is writing about those essential things giving true happiness.

Honours and legacy

From 1993 until the introduction of the Euro Saint-Exupéry's portrait and several of his drawings from The Little Prince appeared on France's 50-franc banknote. The French Government also later minted a 100-franc commemorative coin, with Saint-Exupéry on its front and the Little Prince on its reverse. Brass-plated souvenir Monnaie de Paris commemorative medallions were also created in his honour, depicting the pilot's portrait over the P-38 Lightning aircraft he last flew.

In 1999, the Government of Quebec and Quebec City added a historical marker to the family home of Charles De Koninck, head of the Department of Philosophy at Universite Laval where the Saint-Exupérys stayed while lecturing in Canada for several weeks during May and June 1942.

Asteroid 2578 Saint-Exupéry, discovered in November 1975 by Russian astronomer Tamara Smirnova and provisionally cataloged as Asteroid 1975 VW3, was renamed in the author-aviator's honour. Another asteroid was named as 46610 Besixdouze (translated to and from both hexadecimal and French as 'B612'). Additionally the terrestrial-asteroid protection organization B612 Foundation was named in tribute to the author's Little Prince who fell to Earth from Asteroid B-612.

Philatic tributes have been printed in at least 25 other countries as of 2011. Only three years after his death, the pilot-aviator was first featured on an 8 franc French West Africa airmail stamp. France followed several months later in 1948 with an 80 franc airmail stamp honouring him and later with another stamp honouring him. In commemoration of the 50th anniversary of the writer's death Israel issued a stamp honoring 'Saint-Ex' and The Little Prince in 1994.

Saint-Exupéry was the only foreign pilot authorized to board the giant Soviet aircraft Tupolev ANT-20 Maxim Gorky.

The forty-fourth class of police commissioners from the École nationale supérieure de la police, which took office in 1994

The theme of the 1967 Montreal World Fair was 'Terre des Hommes'.

One of the French Air Force squadrons Saint-Exupéry flew with, adopted the image of the The Little Prince as part of the squadron and tail insignia on its Dassault Mirage Fighter jets.

Google celebrated Saint-Exupéry's 110th birthday with a special logotype depicting the little prince being hoisted through the heavens by a flock of birds.

Uruguayan airline BQB Lineas Aereas named one of its aircraft, an ATR-72 in honor of the aviator.

International Watch Company (IWC) has created many St Exupery tribute versions of several of their wristwatch lines, with the distinctive 'A' from his signature featured on the dial.

The American aviation magazine Flying ranked Saint-Exupéry number 41 on their list of the 51 Heroes of Aviation.

Orson Welles had bought the rights of the Little Prince and had proposed to Walt Disney to adapt it in animation. After reading it, Disney said there was no room for two geniuses in the business.

The B612 Foundation is a private non profit foundation headquartered in Mill Valley, California dedicated to planetary science and defence against asteroids impacts. It is led mainly by scientists, former astronauts and engineers from the Institute for Advanced Study, Stanford University, NASA and the space industry. The B612 Foundation is named for the asteroid home of the eponymous hero of The Little Prince.

In aviation's early pioneer years of the 1920s, Saint-Exupéry made an emergency landing on top of an African mesa covered with crushed white limestone seashells. Walking around in the moonlight he kicked a black rock and soon deduced it was a meteorite that had fallen from space. That experience later contributed, in 1943, to his literary creation of Asteroid B-612 in his philosophical fable of a little prince fallen to Earth, with the home planetoid's name having been adapted from one of the mail planes Saint-Exupéry once flew, bearing the registration marking A-612.

OCTOBER 31, 2016
Canadian Prime Minister Justin Trudeau and his family went all-out for Halloween, with detailed costumes for their trick-or-treating. Trudeau, dressed as the pilot from The Little Prince complemented his youngest son, who dressed as the Prince. Trudeau's other

children went as the Joker and a witch, while his wife, Sophie Trudeau, wore a spooky black dress. Guess that's how they do it up in Canada.

Saint-Exupery on Stamps

<u>Argentina</u>
October 31 1929 Envelope carried and signed by Saint-Ex on first official Comodoro Rivadavia - Trelew airmail flight
July 13 1985 historic flight covers Envelope carried and signed by Saint-Ex Bahia Blanca - Comodoro Rivadavia, Nov 1929
June 3 1995 Aerofila souvenir sheet
October 30 1999 St-Exupéry's Laté 25 F-AIEH
July 29 2000 1900-1944 Antoine de Saint-Exupéry 25¢ text in Spanish, English, French
2000 Birth Centenary privately printed labels for a philatelic dealers' bourse in Buenos Aires,
<u>Bulgaria</u> June 20 2000 birth centenary
<u>Cameroun</u> May 20 1977 airmail pioneers
<u>Central African Republic</u> 1994 50th anniversary of the death of St-Ex
<u>Chad</u> October 25 1978 75th anniversary of powered flight
March 15 1984 Saint-Ex on souvenir sheet background
<u>Comoros</u> 2008 Aviators including Saint-Exupéry, Charles Lindbergh
<u>Congo</u> 2006 Great Aviators including - Saint-Ex
<u>Croatia</u> September 20 1994 50th anniversary of the death of St-Ex
<u>Croatia</u> July 2 1999 PhilexFrance 99 postcard
<u>Djibouti</u> October 7 1983 50th Anniversary of Air France souvenir sheet on wood St-Exupéry
<u>Equitorial Guinea</u> 1994 famous men
<u>France</u> January 19 1948 engraved by Pierre Gandon
September 19 1970 aviators Saint-Exupéry (1900-44)
May 28 1994 aerogramme
September 12 1998 The Little Prince PhilexFrance Paris, July 2-11 1999
June 24 2000 Centenary of the birth of St-Ex

French West Africa March 24 1947 "Courrier Sua 1928"
Gabon 1994 50th anniversary of the death of St-Ex
1996 Saint-Exupéry French cultural centre
Germany 2014 little prince
Grenada 2002 International Year of Mountains
Granada Grenadines March 15 1978 France 1970 C43 Saint-Ex
Guinea 2008 homage to Homage to Georges Guynemer (Saint-Ex photo on souvenir sheet)
2008 The Little Prince "Means of transportation in popular culture"
2014 70th Anniversary of the death of Saint Ex
April 1 1994 50th anniversary of the death of St-Ex [Little Prince]
Israel June 21 1994 50th anniversary of the death of St-Ex [Little Prince]
September 11 2012 The Little Prince sheetlet Holidays, Hannukah
Korea April 22 2025 Information and Communication of the Future, Little Prince with Sheep and Rose
Mexico October 6 1994 50th anniversary of the death of St-Ex
Morocco 1994 50th anniversary of the death of St-Ex
November 13 2000 Centenary of the birth of St-Ex
Mozambique 2002 Saint-Exupéry, Lindberg, Concorde ss sheet block of 4
New Caledonia July 7 2000 Centenary of the birth of St-Ex
Poland June 1 2005 The Little Prince sheet block of four
Russia Aug 16 2005 The Earth: Deep Blue Planet (with St-Ex quotation: "Water")
Sao Tome Principe 2006 Great World Aeronautical Events souvenir sheet: Saint-Ex - Dbs 5000
Senegal August 30 1989 St-Ex novels Courrier Sud (1929) Vol de Nuit (1931) Pilote de Guerre (1942)
Sierra Leone June 29 2018 75th anniversary of publication of Little Prince

<u>Slovakia</u> May 25 1994 50th anniversary of the death of St-Ex
<u>Wallis & Futuna</u> October 27 1994 50th anniversary of the death of St-Ex
<u>Zanzibar</u> 2014 Cinderellas (70th anniversary of the death of St-Ex)
2016 Cinderellas (Little Prince sculpture at Abakan)

The Little Prince in popular culture

Film

The Little Prince 1966

A TV movie of The Little Prince behalf of DFF television film by Konrad Wolf. It was an adaptation of Antoine de Saint-Exupéry's modern fairy tale, which first appeared in the GDR in 1965. The backdrops and the costumes remained close to the book's illustrations. Since the content and the text of the book were not falsified for the film, the summary in The Little Prince is correct. The third star drunk and the sixth star explorer were not included in the film.

The Little Prince 1974

British-American fantasy musical film with screenplay and lyrics by Alan Jay Lerner, music by Frederick Loewe. It was both directed and produced by Stanley Donen and based on the 1943 classic children-adult's novella. The film and its music were unsuccessful at the box office but became somewhat popular after its theatrical run, and has been released for sale on various media.

The Adventures of the Little Prince (TV series) 1978

The Adventures of the Little Prince is an anime series based on The Little Prince. Made by the animation studio Knack Productions, the series, originally titled The Prince of the Stars: Le Petit Prince aired in Japan on the TV Asahi network from

July 1978 to March 1979. Dubbed into English, the series premiered in Los Angeles & New York on ABC in 1982, and the rest of the United States in 1985 on Nickelodeon and was rerun through June 1, 1985 to December 29, 1989. It was also broadcast on TV Ontario throughout the 1980s beginning in 1985. In total there were 26 episodes aired in English, with 39 episodes made for the original Japanese run.

The Little Prince 1979

Directed by Will Vinton. The Little Prince questions the universe in this story of innocence and wonder.
One of the very first adaptations of the book on film here, and as such it is a treat to be able to watch it nowadays; some of the versions that preceded it seem to be currently unavailable. This one, the first straight take in the English language as the previous British-American movie (from 1974) was a musical, is pretty faithful to the written text. The art design is colourful and the animation (both clay and watercolor-painted) experimental to a point, although the whole thing feels too abstract for its 25-plus minutes of length and its target audience. Somehow, the solitude exuded by the source work gets conveyed through those means, though, as if the film had been pictured directly from a character's sun-damaged imagination. Cliff Robertson voices the pilot narrator stranded in the desert --curiously enough, Robertson (who, like Saint-Exupéry, was a real-life aviator) would star in the cult aviation flick The Pilot just the following year--, lending a timely gravitas and credibility to an otherwise understandably limited affair, as Le petit prince is definitely one of the very greatest fictions ever conceived.

Wings of Courage, 1995

Docudrama by French director Jean-Jacques Annaud. The movie was the world's first dramatic picture shot in the IMAX-format, and is an account of the true story of early airmail pilots Henri Guillaumet (played by Craig Sheffer), Saint-Exupéry played by Tom Hulce.

Saint-Ex 1997

Saint-Exupéry and his wife Consuelo were portrayed by Bruno Ganz and Miranda Richardson in the 1997 biopic Saint-Ex a British film biography of the French author-pilot. It was filmed and distributed in the United Kingdom, with scripting by Frank Cottrell Boyce.

The Little Prince 2015

A 2015 English-language French-Italian animated family drama directed by Mark Osborne. The film stars the voices of Jeff Bridges and Ricky Gervais. It is the first adaptation as a full-length animated feature of The Little Prince. The film relates the story of the book using animation about a young girl who has just met the book's now-elderly aviator narrator, who tells her the story of his meeting with the Little Prince. The film premiered on 22 May 2015 at the Cannes Film Festival followed by a wide release in France on 29 July. The film was originally set to be released in theatres across the United States on March 18, 2016 before being dropped due to budget cuts. Netflix later acquired the US distribution rights and released it on August 5, 2016. The film has received positive reviews, earning praise for its style of animation and homage paid to the source material, and earned $97.6 million on a €55 million budget, becoming the most successful French animated film abroad of all time.

Invisible Essence: The Little Prince 2018
Written & Diected by Charles Officer
1h 30min Documentary March 2019 Canada

Antoine de Saint-Exupéry's transcendent story suggests an ethical philosophy about life and a universal code of respect for humanity. With every new generation that discovers the fable, the Little Prince's inspiring legacy is cemented.

The film refers to and includes clips from four dramatizations of the book. These are The Little Prince, 1974, a live action musical feature film, directed by Stanley Donen with music by Lerner and Loewe; a 1975 Grammy-winning audio version read by Richard Burton; The Little Prince, 2015, a live action and stop-motion animated feature film directed by Mark Osborne; and Le Petit Prince, 2016, a ballet created by Guillaume Coté for the National Ballet of Canada.

Other film & television adaptations

1966: A Soviet Lithuanian adaption
1966: The German DDR network broadcasts a TV movie of Der Kleine Prinz by Konrad Wolf
1976: James Dean, Directed by Robert Buttler, pages of the novel are read out by Dean played by Stephen McHattie.
1978: The Adventures of the Little Prince, a Japanese animated aired in Europe and North America in the 1970s and 1980s. During the 1980s, the English-language version was aired in the United States.
1978: A Russian animated series The Adventures of the Little Prince produced by Franklin Kofod.
1979: A Claymation short film adaptation titled The Little Prince created by Will Vinton written by Susan Shadburne, featuring Cliff Robertson as the narrator-pilot.

1990: A 60-minute German ZDF annimated film, Der Kleine Prinz produced by Theo Kerp.
1990: A French film adaptation is released as Le Petit Prince by Jean Louis Guillermou.
2001: The film Picture Claire starring Juliette Lewis and Callum Keith Rennie includes several references, including animations, to The Little Prince.
2003: In The Walt Disney TV movie Eloise at the Plaza, The Little Prince played an important part in the Prince's plot. His mother read the book to him and several quotes from the book appeared in the movie as well.
2004: An operatic adaptation based on the music of Rachel Portman (featuring Willard White and Lesley Garrett was broadcast on the UK's BBC2 television network on 27 November 2004 as a studio-filmed production starring Joseph McManners as The Prince and Teddy Tahu Rhodes as The Pilot, and later released as a DVD.
2010: Le Petit Prince title of Computer animated TV series of 52 episodes of 26 minutes each by Method Animation. The Little Prince is voiced by Gabriel Bismuth-Bienaimé,
2011: Oliver d'Agay of the Saint-Exupéry–d'Agay Estate, responsible for author's intellectual property and head of the Antoine de Saint-Exupéry Youth Foundation, reached an agreement with the author's original French publisher and others on creating updated adaptations of The Little Prince story. In the new adaptations The Prince is made more attuned to children of the 21st century and include a new 3D animated movie, as well as an animated TV series in 52 parts, The Little Prince (2010 TV series), a new video game, and 100 serial print story editions. The TV series is produced in collaboration with France Télévisions, TV5 Monde, the Swiss Television and the Italian Rai Fiction, and licensed for distribution in many countries worldwide. The animated movie is titled as Le Petit Prince 4D, produced by nWave Pictures, with effects by Parc

du Futuroscope.
2011: Der Kleine Prinz is produced for DVD in Berlin, directed by Lorenz Christian Köhler.
2012: The Little Prince TV series was translated into Scottish Gaelic.

Music and cultural references

1974: Genesis initial concept for their 1974 album that became The Lamb Lies Down on Broadway was initially The Little Prince.
1975, Yonatan Geffen wrote a song called The Little Prince telling about a soldier who served alongside him and was killed during a combat exercise. The song contains numerous allusions to the book.
1979: The Russian rock band Mashina Vremeni played a concert program in 1979–80, called The Little Prince and included intersong quotations from the book. The whole concept of the program (the live version was released in 2000) was based on the story and the philosophy of the book.
1994: Le Petit Prince a La Geode, multimedia show with music by Giuseppe Verdi was produced by Gianni Ravens and Pierre Goismier at the Geode Music Hall in Paris, France
1997: An orchestral suite is conducted by Nicholas Schapfl in Shanghai,China
1999: Jana Kirschner, a lead slovak singer has a song 'Fox', named after a character from the book. The lyrics of the song deal with the relationship between The Little Prince and The Fox.
2002: The cover art of the Japanese band P-Model album Perspective was inspired by the book; the album also includes the song A Large Snake whose lyrics also reference the book.
2002: The U.S. Screamo band The Saddest Landscape takes their name from the closing passage of The Little Prince and

one of their songs, 'Forty Four Sunsets', refers to one of the book's episodes.
2006: French singer Mylene Farmer recorded a song, 'Dessine-moi un Mouton' ("Draw me a sheep"), which alludes to The Little Prince.
2006: Singer–pianist Regina Spektor has a song entitled 'Baobabs', which refers to The Little Prince and the effect it has on its readers. The song entitled "Baobabs" was included in their special edition vinyl album, Begin to Hope, released in June 2006.
2008: The Taiwanese female group band S.H.E. released a song entitled "Planet 612", which pays tribute to The Little Prince.
2010: JimmyThumP/OneRoomSong composed a Vocaloid song entitled "Little Traveler", that is based on the story.
2012: sasakure.UK composed a song entitled "to asteroid B-612", that is based on the story.
2015: Prog band Riverside drew inspiration from The Little Prince when writing opening track Lost (Why Should I Be Frightened By a Hat?) on their album Love Fear and The Time Machine.
2016: The Korean singer Kim Ryeowook of idol group Super Junior released his first solo minialbum entitled 'The Little Prince' which features the lead single of the same name.
Saint-Exupéry's death and speculation that Horst Rippert shot him down are the subject of 'Saint Ex', a song on Widespread Panic's eleventh studio album, Dirty Side Down.
The Norwegian progressive rock band Gazpacho's concept album Tick Tock is based on Saint-Exupéry's desert crash.
'On the Planet of the Living', a song sung by Eduard Khil, was dedicated to Saint-Exupéry.
'St. Exupéry Blues' – a song by Russian folk-rock band Melnitsa from their album "Alchemy"

Audio adaptations Vinyl record

1954: An audio adaptation, as a vinyl record, was made with the French actor Gerard Philipe in the role of The Narrator, Georges Poujouly.
1956: A German adaption on a Philips label double LP record album, narrated by Hardy Krüger
1972: An adaptation with Jean-Louis Trintignant in the role of narrator and Eric Damain in the role of The Prince
1972: An adaption withPeter Ustinov reading all roles.
1973: An adaptation with Marcel Mouloudji in the role of narrator and Eric Remy in the role of The Prince.
1975: Actor Richard Burton won the Grammy Award for Best Album for Children for his narration of The Little Prince featuring Jonathan Winters, Claude Longet and Billy Simpson. It was produced by Buddy Kaye with music by Mort Garson.
1978: A phono adaptation with Jean-Claude Pascal in the role of narrator was released.
1983: Songs from the German version,Der Kleine Prinz by Kurt Demmler, and later produced in 1985 as a double LP on the Amiga label
1990: A phono adaptation with Pierre Arditi in the role of narrator and Benjamin Pascal in the role of The Prince was released.
1996: A Digital Quebec production with a musical score by Robert Normandeau was released. Actor Michel Dumont as the Narrator–Aviator.

Radio broadcasts

1953: An adaptation by Jon Farrell, with incidental music composed by James Bernard was broadcast on the BBC Light Programme on 20 December 1953.
1956:Raymond Burr starred in a radio adaptation of The Little Prince on The CBS Radio Workshop.

1974: Jon Farrell's adaptation, with Nigel Stock as Narrator and Gwyn Guthrie as The Little Prince, was broadcast on 13 April 1974 on BBC Radio 4.

1999: BBC Radio 4 broadcast, on Christmas Day 1999 (and subsequently repeated), a dramatisation by Bonnie Greer of a new translation into English of The Little Prince Produced by Pam Fraser Solomon, and with music composed by Keith Waithe the dramatization starred Robert Powell as the aviator and narrator, Garrett Moore as The Little Prince, and Bernard Cribbins as The King, The Drunkard, and The Lamplighter. It was repeated in May 2002. An audio cassette recording is available in the BBC Radio Collection series.

Cassette tape and CD

1959: An audio cassette adaptation in German, with Will Quadflieg in the role of narrator.

1994: Adapted to a CD, by Matthew Mancini and others, with music by Fabio Concato, directed by Marco Carniti, on the EMI label from Milan Italy in 1994

1996: Marc André Coallier narrated Le Petit Prince supported by Marc-André Grondin, Sophie Stanké, Paul Buissoneau, Ghislain Tremblay, Gaston Lepage, Jean-Pierre Gonthier and Gilbert Lachance. The accompanying music was performed by Alexandre Stanké.

1998: A CD adaptation is directed by Romain Victo-Pujebet, with rumors of Philippe Leroy, with original music by Olivier Priszlak, released in Paris by Gallimard and in Milan by Pontaccio.

1999: An audiobook adaptation on the Patmos label, read by Ulrich Muhe

2009: Horbuch von Rausch (Ecstasy Audiobook) adaptation of Der Kleine Prinz with a new translation narrated by Jan Josef Liefers.

Ballet

1982: Malenkiy Prints ballet with the music of Belarussian composer Yevgeniy Glebov.
1985: Der Kleine Prinz ballet is performed by the Gregor Seyffert Company in Dessau, Germany
1987: The Los Angeles Chamber Ballet produced The Little Prince for two performances at the Orange County Performing Arts Centre in Costa Mesa, California.
2010: The Ballet d'Europe performed The Little Prince in a new ballet choreographed by Florencia Gonzalez and performed by nine dancers, with a score by René Aubry.
2012: Les Grands Ballets Canadiens produced the story as ballet, performed at Montreal's Place Des Arts venue.
2014: The Hurjaruuth Dance Theatre, Helsinki created a new production, with direction by Arja Pettersson, expressing the story's elements of friendship, loneliness, the search for happiness and the thrill of life in general.

Operas and musical productions

1964: Russian operatic composer Lev Knipper wrote a three-part symphony in 1962, entitled Malenkiy Prints (The Little Prince) which was first performed in Moscow in 1978.
1981: A musical theatre adaptation entitled The Little Prince and the Aviator co-produced by lawyer A. Joseph Tandet who held the rights to The Little Prince with music composed by John Barry and directed by Jerry Adler.
1985: Der Kleine Prinz opera with music by Michael Horwath and libretto by Barbara Hass.
2002: Le Petit Prince as a musical comedy by Richard Cocciante.

2003: Rachel Portman composed an English opera The Little Prince based on the book that had its stage premiere in 2003 at the Houston Grand Opera starring Nate Irvin as The Prince, receiving widespread critical acclaim. It was broadcast on the UK's BBC Two television network on November 27, 2004, as a studio-filmed production starring Joseph McManners as The Prince.
2003: Opera composer Nikolaus Schapfl composes Der Kleine Prinz in German,after first obtaining the rights from the author's heirs in 1998. As of 2007, it has been performed 25 times in seven other European cities by five different orchestras and ensembles. In 2005, it was broadcast by Bavarian Classic Radio.
2015: A new musical version in German of "The Little Prince" produced by 3for1 Trinity Concerts GmbH in Lorsch, Germany, premiered at the Musical Theater Niedernhausen (Wiesbaden) on December 12/2015.
2016: A new musical version of The Little Prince produced by Theatre Calgary, Canada.

Live theatre dramas

1950: The first German theatrical adaptation of Der Kleine Prinz is created by puppeteer Rudolf Fischer.
1971: An Italian theatrical adaptation is produced by Remo Rostagno and Bruna Pilgrims.
1987: Adapted to live theatre in English by David Zucker, produced by Esquire Jauchem and Peter Ellenstein as The Little Prince featuring David Morse and Bridget Hoffman, at the Cast Theatre and Burbage Theatre in Los Angeles.
1994: Adapted to live theatre in Italian featuring Maria Antonietta and Giuseppina Canapa, at the Aperto Theater in Italy
2000: A play adaptation written by Rick Cummins and John

Scoullar.

2002: The French-language musical by composer Riccardo Cocciante ran at the Casino de Paris.

2002: Adapted to a live theatre play by Anja Pirling, herself playing the main part of "The little prince". Opening night in the Circus Krone Munich, than touring for 6 years in more than 140 cities (concert halls and theatres with up to 2000 seats) in Germany.

2005: Peter Joucla adapted and directed a version for Tour de Force Theatre which toured Germany.

2008: The Little Prince was staged as a solo play by Indian actress Rashi Bunny and adapted to Hindi by Capt. Rigved

2008: The Hampstead Theatre in London produced a theatre adaptation.

2008: A French theater adaptation with interactive video produced by the group Theatre Trois Hangars.

2011: The Portuguese drama company Byfurcação produces a theatrical adaptation.

2011: The Oxford University Dramatic Society tour of a new translation and adaptation of the book to the Edinburgh Fringe Festival.

2011: Serbian director Srdjan Simic produces a Russian language adaptation in Moscow.

2012: The Dragonfly Theatre Co. put on an original adaptation in Ho Chi Minh City, Vietnam.

2015: Bossy Flyer created an acrobatic theatre adaptation called Flight. Adapted and directed by Ezra LeBank, premiered at the 2015 Edinburgh Festival Fringe, and was performed Off-Broadway at the Barrow Street Theatre in New York City in September 2016.

2016: Christine Lesiak created a radical, site-specific, adaptation titled The Object of Constellations in which the character of the pilot is recast as an female astronomer. It premiered April 2016 in Edmonton, Canada.

2017: Théâtre du Rêve staged a new French-language adaptation by Carolyn Cook in Atlanta, Georgia

Who Owns Le Petit Prince?

In much of the world, currently, heirs to a dead author enjoy rights associated with his or her works for 50 years, after which the writings are considered to be in the public domain. In the European Union, the term is 70 years, as a result of legal harmonisation agreed upon in 1993. As Saint-Exupery died in 1944, his works should have become freely available on January 1st 2015, though they were already considered to be in the public domain in countries like India or Morocco which are not as generous in their protection of literary property rights as European law. In the U.K. or Ireland for instance, The Little Prince has indeed been out of copyright for over a year. The same does not hold true for France.

Before the EU came to an agreement regarding the time during which works would be protected, France applied a duration of 50 years post mortem but also had a special clause for those who had lived through one or other of the world wars (or both): the war years were deemed to count twice, so for 'Saint-Ex' as he is affectionately known, you need to add 8 years and 120 days to the 50 years everyone was granted. In addition, as Saint-Exupery was engaged in active service, he is deemed to have died for his country, 'mort pour la France' is the official designation, which means a 30 year gratification is granted. Result: (50+8+30) years+120 days, added to 1944, means that, as there is no retroactive application of the 70 year rule, Saint-Exupery's texts will only come into the 'domaine public' in France in... April 2033.

Copyright on The Little Prince would have expired in 2014, 70 years after the author's death in 1944. But his widow, and inheritor of the copyright, Consuelo de Saint-Exupéry, renewed the copyright in 1971, which extends it to 2041. The

Succession Saint Exupéry - d'Agay represents the heirs and assigns of Antoine de Saint Exupéry, his 4 nephews, the children of his sister Gabrielle. The missions of the Succession are to spread the work of their uncle around the world, by all means, to transmit their humanist values to new generations and to put their reputation at the service of the community.

About the author

Johnny Wallman was born in Manchester in 1962. He worked retail for over forty years, lived in Israel working in hotels and serving in the Israeli army, and owned and ran a bed and breakfast in Annan, South Scotland. Retired, he now lives in Bacup, Lancashire. He has known The Little Prince for over forty years, once tamed, now friends forever.

'Look up at the sky and ask yourself 'Has the sheep eaten the flower or not?' And you will see how everything changes... And no grown up will ever understand how such a thing could be so important'.

Milton Keynes UK
Ingram Content Group UK Ltd.
UKHW020801250224
438379UK00013B/1400